Westside

CHRONICLES

Westside
CHRONICLES

Historic Stories of West Los Angeles

JAN LOOMIS

THE History PRESS

Published by The History Press
Charleston, SC 29403
www.historypress.net

Unless otherwise noted, all images are from the Santa Monica Land & Water Company archives.

First published 2012

Manufactured in the United States

ISBN 978.1.60949.623.4

Library of Congress CIP data applied for.

Notice: The information in this book is true and complete to the best of our knowledge. It is offered without guarantee on the part of the author or The History Press. The author and The History Press disclaim all liability in connection with the use of this book.

For all of those who will come after and create their own stories about West Los Angeles—may they maintain what has been done as they build their own vision across the area for its future residents.

Contents

Acknowledgements

In doing the research for this book, it became apparent that there is considerable overlap between every part of West Los Angeles (WLA) and its history. Even today, the original five ranchos remain a potent influence on the land and its use. The original developers competed against and inspired each other. They shared many common goals. The homeowners brought ideas from former homes and other areas. The architects influenced each other and the styles of homes and buildings worldwide; the athletes who used the beach clubs and swam in the surf went on to compete on the international stage. Surfing slang invented on these beaches is heard everywhere. The movies using WLA as a backdrop impacted viewers across the nation and the world.

However, no one book or article has tried to tell the saga of West Los Angeles (as defined by the five ranchos that define the area) as a whole—to show the way each developer influenced the others; how the landscape reflects their joint interests and their joint goals; how the decisions of one affected all of the others. How the weather and the perpetual resort environment determined the look and feel of the area. How popular sports shaped its development. How much WLA has influenced the rest of the country and the world.

This book is an attempt to show these connections and interactions in a way that helps the reader see the bigger picture and understand why West Los Angeles has become such an important part of Los Angeles and such an influence on the nation and the world. It tells the story of the players, the landscape, the builders, the streets, the amusements and the impact of the early movie industry.

Acknowledgements

Much of the information for this book was found in the Santa Monica Land & Water Company archives (SML&WCo)—a large repository of business papers, photographs, ephemera and other records about business in West Los Angeles. Local history books about Pacific Palisades, Brentwood, Playa del Rey and Santa Monica offered many helpful insights. Articles written for *Previews* magazine and other local publications by local writers were also very helpful. So were the online histories of the various institutions and historic sites located in West Los Angeles.

My heartfelt gratitude to those who personally helped me piece together this story and the images used to illustrate it, especially: Dorothy Gillis Loomis, Arthur Loomis, Adelaide Gillis McCormick, Peggy Loomis and Francis McCormick Armstrong. Their firsthand accounts and memories of events have been invaluable. Lois Flagg deserves much gratitude for preserving the SML&WCo archives through thick and thin over her fifty-five-year career with the company. Local historians Betty Lou Young and Randy Young's books are important resources on several Westside areas; Ernie Marquez's books are a treat to look at and provide valuable information about his family and Santa Monica Bay. Dace Taube, archivist at the University of Southern California Libraries, and Cynni Murphy, at the Santa Monica Public Library, were both invaluable resources for information and images. Please see the bibliography for a complete list of books and sources used for research.

Finally, special thanks to my husband, Bob Loomis, for his meticulous research about the various families who developed West Los Angeles and their relationships; for his help with the SML&WCo archive research; for his ability to scan a photo or tract map; and finally, for his patient reading of the drafts of this book and for his many suggestions and improvements. It could not have been done without you.

The sweep of this book is broad, and while I have done my best to get it right, I'm sure there are errors. Please let me know about any mistakes so that I can correct the record.

Introduction

We all do it—drive the streets, go in and out of the buildings, navigate the curves, enjoy the beach, love the weather, find pleasure in the views, jog and walk on the streets, enjoy the tennis, golf and surfing—but we don't spend any time at all wondering how it all got there. Who picked the names for the streets; why are the curves and intersections where they are; who created the homes and buildings; who first saw the views; who first played tennis and golf on Westside courts and courses; who made surfing popular.

Although it is hard to believe today, West Los Angeles was once more than sixty-eight thousand acres of open land—scrub brush, running streams, a few trees, small game and dust. Native Americans roamed it first and then gave way to the rancheros who brought their cattle, horses and agriculture to the land. Neither group changed the landscape much; it remained mostly open space. Then the capitalists and the promoters arrived and began to transform the land into neighborhoods and communities. In the process, they added infrastructure, landscaping and new contours to the geography. Their vision changed the open land into the West Los Angeles of today—an affluent suburb, home to over a quarter million people who live, work and play in pleasant towns and neighborhoods.

The names are recognizable, memorialized in street names, on beach signs, on monuments and in the names of the communities they built. The land conforms to their visions, and the recreation and sports facilities they created are important reasons to live in West Los Angeles, but the stories of how it all came about are gone from local memory.

In order to tell these tales, it was necessary to reconstruct the sequence of events and the intertwined relationships of the people who shaped the area.

Five ranchos were granted to five different family groups. They were the first to alter the landscape, and the contours of their ranchos still shape West Los Angeles today. The ranchero families intermarried with each other and with other Californio families, tying the area to Los Angeles. The sales of their land to the capitalists began the next phase of the area's development. The buyers were also friends and associates and had family ties to each other. They worked together, and their names appear over and over on the letterheads, deeds, tract maps and legal papers related to the development of West Los Angeles.

Common themes emerged as the story began to develop. At first, the land's distance from Los Angeles and the San Gabriel and San Fernando Missions was an advantage. The priests were not able to interfere with the owners, and the city had little interest in the area. Later, the distance worked against the developers, especially during the Great Depression. Then it was an asset again as LA dropped under a murky cloud of smog. The weather in West Los Angeles is spectacular—cooled by sea breezes and dewed by fog, with mild temperatures and many days of sunshine. The everyday resort environment attracted a steady stream of residents, even during Los Angeles's historic real estate busts. The health benefits of the mild climate drew many residents from other areas of the country—asthma and other respiratory ailments persuaded both residents and developers to live and invest in the area. The climate engendered a yen for outdoor sports and encouraged an open architecture for homes. Plants thrived, and horticulture was a popular hobby. The area quickly became a lush garden environment. The movies discovered the weather and added their glitz and glamour to the region. All these advantages led to ever-increasing real estate values for the land.

It has all added up over the last one-hundred-plus years to a rich mix of people, places and activities. West Los Angeles is a name that evokes vibrant people, neighborhoods, communities and towns that provide ideas and trends to influence the country and the world. Enjoy the tales about how it came to be.

Chapter 1
THE PLAYERS

Many individuals contributed to the development of West Los Angeles in many different ways. Their names repeat throughout the area on streets, buildings, documents, monuments and parks. Some of them were born in other countries, many came from other states and many were born in California or in West Los Angeles. They were often related to each other or married into each other's families. They shared the good times and the bad times; made money together; lost money on each other's projects; and competed against each other in tennis, polo and golf and in business. Meet the players, and follow them through their careers as they developed West Los Angeles from open land to suburb.

Native Americans

First the Chumash tribes lived along the coastal regions of California from San Luis Obispo to Malibu. They built canoes for travel and traded up and down the coast. The Gabrielino Tongva tribes were also among the first people to enjoy the vistas and hills of West Los Angeles. One of their villages was near the Kuruvunga Springs (today University High School). The name means "a place where we are in the sun," which seems appropriate for the area. However, grinding stones for turning acorns into meal have been found at different locations all around the region. The mouth of Sullivan Canyon yielded a small fired-clay female figure. A site in Topanga Canyon was excavated in the 1940s, and several thousand pounds of artifacts were recovered. It was the first habitation site found that contained enough information to give a picture of these early inhabitants. They were hunter-gatherers who made primitive stone tools and baskets. There would have been abundant water, acorns, wild berries, fish and birds for drink and food, as well as a temperate climate. Shell beads were used as currency, and life would have been an endless round of following the seasons and the food.

Explorers

Spain sent explorers to survey the lands it claimed and also to find trading opportunities. A succession of explorers made forays north of "New Spain" (Mexico) from 1530 through the 1700s. In 1540, Juan Rodriquez Cabrillo, a wealthy conquistador, was commissioned by the viceroy of New Spain, Antonio de Mendoza, to explore the Pacific Coast and look for trade routes to Asia. Cabrillo sailed up the coast exploring the bays and coast of what had been called California (probably because of the fantastic tales told of its riches). According to accounts, he dropped his anchor in Santa Monica Bay and spent the night there. Other expeditions explored the coast of California, but there is no record of further contact with the West Los Angeles area until Jose de Galvez, visitor general for New Spain, organized a four-part expedition in 1769 to explore and colonize the area designated as Alta California. His immediate goal was to protect the northern frontier of New Spain from Russian and British encroachment.

Gaspar de Portola

Gaspar de Portola led one of the land expeditions that Galvez commissioned. Portola was a Spanish soldier who became the governor of Alta and Baja California. His land expedition was charged with colonizing Alta California for Spain and preventing English and Russian expansion into the area. Father Junipero Serra was part of the expedition and was charged with setting up a series of missions to convert the Indians to Christianity. Once Portola had established the Presidio of San Diego, he started north hoping to find Monterey Bay (described in glowing terms by earlier explorer Sebastian Vizcaino). The group—consisting of sixty-three soldiers, one hundred mules and Father Juan Crespi, the record keeper for the expedition—followed the Indian trail along the hills (now Wilshire Boulevard) and camped near the Tongva village and the Kuruvunga Springs. Several names for the springs were documented in their writings, such as San Vicente, El Berrendo, San

Gregorio and Santa Monica. They turned inland from the springs and went north through the Sepulveda Pass. The Santa Monica name does not appear until the first grazing grant was made in 1828.

Juan Bautista de Anza

Juan Bautista de Anza was born in Sonora, Mexico, and entered the army in 1752. He explored much of Arizona before becoming interested in California. The sea route to Alta California was dangerous and resulted in heavy losses of ships to storms and sailors to scurvy. A safer overland route was needed from Mexico to California. De Anza found an Indian who had fled from the Mission San Gabriel to Sonora who knew of such a route, and he became his guide. De Anza's expedition left Sonora in January 1774 and reached San Gabriel Mission in March 1774. From there, he went north to Monterey, following the same route that Portola followed.

Fernando Rivera y Moncada

Fernando Rivera y Moncada also led one of the land expeditions sent by Galvez and arrived in San Diego on May 14, 1769. He joined Portola when he started north, exploring with him the Los Angeles, Santa Monica, Santa Barbara and Monterey areas. Rivera was governor of Alta California and led several overland expeditions to Los Angeles, including one in 1781. He was killed by an Indian attack near present-day Yuma during this expedition.

Rancheros

Many of the soldiers of Portola's and other expeditions decided to stay in Alta California when their enlistments were up or when they reached retirement age. As a reward for their service, the Spanish crown allowed them to apply for permission to use parcels of land for grazing and agriculture. Under Spanish law, all land belonged to the crown, and the settlers were only given the concession to use it. After the successful Mexican Revolution in 1821, the laws were changed to make landownership possible. Settlers were required to survey their land, submit a *diseño* (a hand-drawn topographical map) and accept the conditions laid out by the government. They were not allowed to subdivide or rent the land. They each had to build a house and graze a herd of 150 cattle, and they could not close any roads that crossed the

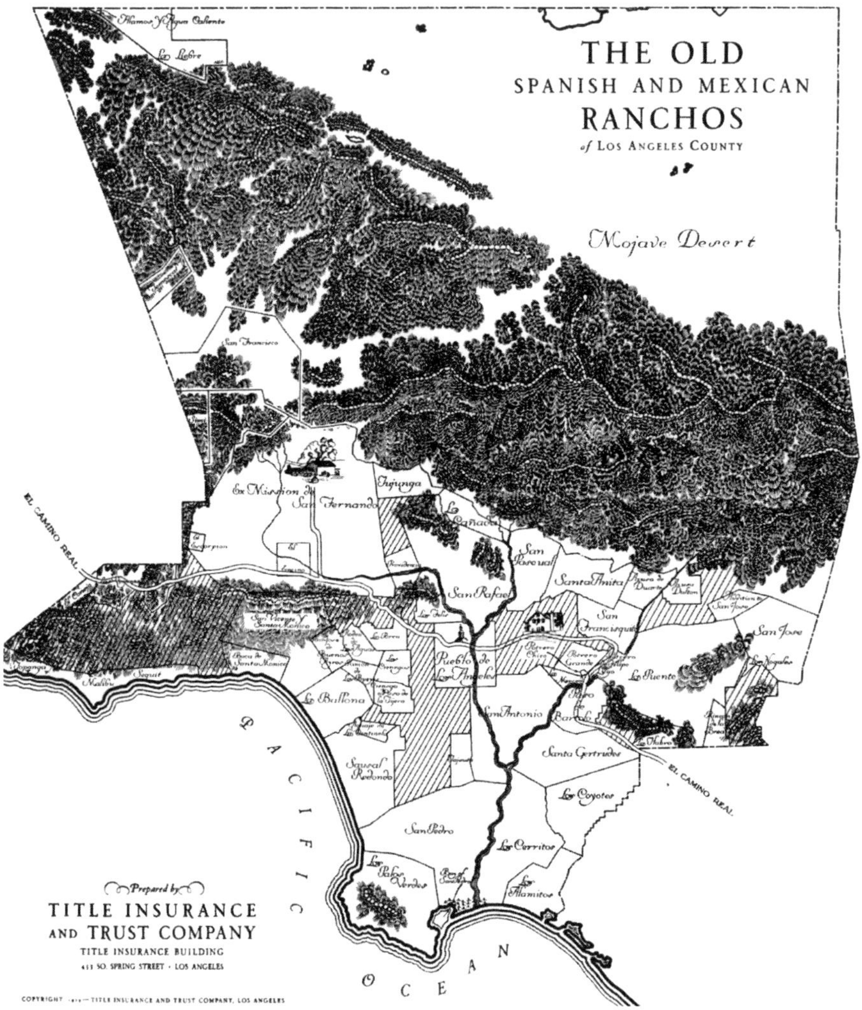

The boundaries of the original five land grants are visible on this 1919 map of the Los Angeles area. *Courtesy of the University of Southern California on behalf of the USC Special Collections.*

property. The soldiers had a preference for land as far as possible from the missions and pueblos (towns). The priests and pueblos had a reputation for interference and confrontation with those living close to them.

Five groups of soldiers received concessions or grants of land to graze their cattle around Santa Monica Bay in the West Los Angeles area. Early Americans in California became rancheros when they purchased the rights to these large blocks of land from the Californios.

Tapia

Jose Bartolome Tapia was born in Culiacan, Sonora, New Spain, and he was about eight years old when he accompanied his father on the de Anza expedition in 1774. (The soldiers of these expeditions were often accompanied by their wives and children.) The de Anza expedition diaries document that they made camp on February 22, 1724, "beside a creek in a grove of oak trees." The area is known today as Malibu Creek. As a grown man and as a reward for his own army service, Tapia asked for the land where he had camped as a child. His concession for Rancho Topanga Malibu Sequit was approved in 1804, making it the earliest in the Santa Monica Bay area. Tapia built an adobe on Vaquero Flats (north of Point Dume) and, at his death in 1824, left to his wife in his will "the vineyard with the planting ground. To carry on the vineyard, let her have the still, the kettle, two pipes and three barrels. All the saints are for my old woman, the mill and the house, and ranch and all the cattle belong to said wife."

Jose Tapia's son, Tiburcio Tapia, was a prosperous merchant and became *alcalde* (mayor) of Los Angeles in 1830 and again in 1837. He served jointly with Jose Loreto Sepulveda. His daughter married Leon Victor Prudhomme, a young Frenchman who worked for Tiburcio. Jose Tapia's widow sold Prudhomme and her daughter the rancho for four hundred pesos, two hundred pesos in cash and two hundred pesos in provisions and wine. Prudhomme prospered on the ranch, selling cattle to the miners searching for gold in Northern California. However, Prudhomme was never able to obtain clear the title to the Rancho Malibu (probably because of its original status as a concession) and sold it to Mathew Keller in 1857.

Keller

Mathew Keller was born and raised in Ireland. He left Ireland and spent time in Texas and Mexico before settling in Los Angeles in 1851. In Los Angeles he was known as "Don Mateo" Keller. He owned real estate, ran a store, was a pioneer vintner and served as a city councilman and county administrator for the growing city. He bought the disputed Rancho Malibu grant for ten cents an acre knowing there was not a clear title, but he was eventually able to obtain a patent. One of the trails in the Santa Monica Mountain Park—the Rising Sun Trail—commemorates his name for the rancho. Agriculture was one of his interests, and he experimented with many plants and trees to see what would grow successfully in the Los Angeles area. One of his other interests was

Matthew Keller purchased the Rancho Malibu from the original grantees and established a house and vineyard. After his death, his son sold the rancho to Frederick Rindge. *Courtesy of the University of Southern California on behalf of the USC Special Collections.*

the Pioneer Oil Company. It was formed to sell asphaltum and coal oil from the La Brea Tar Pits and other natural seeps for waterproofing roofs and boats.

His son, Henry Workman Keller, sold the rancho to Frederick Hastings Rindge for ten dollars an acre in 1891. Keller maintained a small holding in Solstice Canyon, where the Rising Sun Trail is located today. Keller was also a successful businessman in Santa Monica and Los Angeles. The Keller Block he built on Third Street in Santa Monica is still standing and in use. He was president of the Automobile Club of Southern California and spent much of his life promoting a highway that would run from South America to Alaska. He also was instrumental in establishing the Los Angeles zoo.

Machado/Talamantes

Jose Ygnacio Machado was born in the Santa Barbara area in 1797. His parents were part of the Fernando Rivera y Moncada expedition coming from Mexico in 1781. His father was not able to obtain grazing rights for any land during his lifetime, but Jose and his brother Augustin joined forces with Felipe Talamantes and his son Tomas to obtain fourteen thousand acres of land, naming it Rancho La Ballona. The brothers were quite young at this time and undoubtedly needed the partnership with the older Talamantes to acquire the grant. Augustin Machado was a skilled horseman, and he was the rider who staked the claim. The name was perhaps a tribute to Talamantes's family home in Spain—Bayona—or alternatively is a corruption of the Spanish word for whale.

Augustin Machado married Ramona Sepulveda (his second wife) at the Los Angeles Plaza Church in 1827 and eventually had fourteen children with her. The Machados owned the Rancho La Ballona under Spanish, Mexican and American governments. Culver City's Machado Street is named for the family. Ygnacio built the Centinela Adobe in 1834 on another rancho—Aquaje de la Centinela—in present-day Inglewood.

Reyes/Marquez

Francisco Reyes came to California with the Portola expedition. For his service, he was given the concession for the Rancho Encino in today's San Fernando Valley. Reyes was alcalde of Los Angeles from 1793 to 1795. Ysidro Reyes, his grandson, was born in Los Angeles in 1813. (Ysidro's father married into the Machado family in 1808.) Francisco Marquez was a blacksmith. The two men were granted provisional rights to the Rancho Boca de Santa Monica for their herds of cattle in 1839. Reyes was prominent in Los Angeles affairs, although he had a home on the rancho in Rustic Canyon. He was also an early winemaker in the Los Angeles area. Marquez built his home near Santa Monica's

The Marquez adobe was the first house built in Santa Monica Canyon. It was near the Seventh Street Hill and was torn down in the 1920s. *Courtesy of the University of Southern California on behalf of the USC Special Collections.*

Ysidro Reyes (pictured here) and Francisco Marquez established their ownership of the Rancho Boca de Santa Monica in 1839. Reyes built his home near where present-day Sunset Boulevard meets Chautauqua Boulevard. *Courtesy of the University of Southern California on behalf of the USC Special Collections.*

Seventh Avenue and continued to work as a blacksmith. Built in 1839, it was the first house constructed in the area. The two families intermarried, and the Marquez family remains in the area today. The family cemetery located in Santa Monica Canyon is still under their control, making it one of the last pieces of a Mexican land grant still in the original family's hands. The Marquez family encouraged tourists from Los Angeles to use their beachfront property and made Santa Monica Canyon a popular summer destination. Over the years, the rest of the property was sold and resold to various entities, including the Santa Monica Land & Water Company (SML&WCo).

Sepulveda

Francisco Xavier Sepulveda is considered the founder of the Sepulveda family in Alta California, arriving in 1781 as part of Fernando Rivera y Moncada's last expedition. He settled in Los Angeles in 1815 after his service at the Presidio at San Diego. The Sepulveda family owned several large ranchos, including Rancho los Palos Verdes. His son Francisco Sepulveda was born in Sinaloa, Mexico, and was only six when he accompanied his parents to California.

Francisco Sepulveda (Francisco Xavier's son) was granted the Rancho San Vicente y Santa Monica—lands he had been ranching since 1828—in 1839 for his services to the government. His thirteen children eventually all controlled large ranchos. Jose Antonio Andres Sepulveda was a noted horseman and owned the Rancho San Joaquin. His extravagant lifestyle and debts eventually forced him to sell it to James Irvine, Llewellyn Bixby and Thomas Flint.

One of Francisco's daughters married Jose Augustin Antonio Machado (Rancho La Ballona). Other offspring married into prominent California families, including the Avilas, Yorbas, Verdugos, Dominguezes and Carrillos. Jose Antonio Andres Sepulveda's son (Ignacio) was a prominent Los Angeles judge. Francisco Sepulveda's grandchildren sold the Rancho San Vicente y Santa Monica to Robert Symington Baker in 1872. Judge Juan Jose Carrillo, a relative by marriage of F.X. Sepulveda, was a prominent attorney and officeholder in Santa Monica, as well as the father of actor Leo Carrillo, remembered for his role as Pancho in the popular TV program *The Cisco Kid*.

Francisco Xavier Sepulveda was the original owner of the Rancho San Vicente y Santa Monica. His descendants sold the rancho to Robert Symington Baker in 1872. *Courtesy of the University of Southern California on behalf of the USC Special Collections.*

Alanis

Jose Maximo Alanis was one of the Spanish soldiers who accompanied the Rivera y Moncada expedition of 1781 to Los Angeles. He was granted the Rancho San Jose de Buenos Ayres in 1820. He lived on his rancho, naming it "the ranch of the beautiful breezes," grazing horses and cattle until his death in 1851. The rancho was a single league of about 4,400 acres—smaller than the surrounding ranchos—with hills in the north and a flat area in the south. Alanis received legal title to his land in 1843 from the Mexican governor of California after complaining about encroachment by the Sepulvedas on his property. At Alanis's death, the rancho was valued at $600 and sold. It was sold several times before John W. Wolfskill purchased it for $40,000 in 1884.

Wilson

Benjamin Davis Wilson, known as "Don Benito," was a fur trapper who came to Southern California in 1841 with the first American overland settlers. His intent was to go to China, but after spending some time in Southern California, he decided to stay. His first rancho was Jurupa (present-day Riverside). He paid $1,000 for it. Marrying into the Yorba family, he rapidly became a prominent Los Angeles businessman. He owned the Rancho San Pascual (present-day Pasadena, Altadena, South Pasadena, Alhambra, San Marino and San Gabriel). Wilson's daughter married into the Patton family and was the mother of World War II general George S. Patton Jr. In 1851, Wilson was the second elected mayor of Los Angeles after statehood. He loaned money to the owners of both the Rancho Buenos Ayres and La Ballona, acquiring shares of both ranchos through foreclosure. Mount Wilson is named for him.

Wolfskill

John W. Wolfskill, who purchased the Rancho Buenos Ayres from Don Benito Wilson for ten dollars an acre in 1884, was the nephew of William Wolfskill, one of the pioneers of California agriculture. William Wolfskill planted the first citrus grove in California and created the citrus industry, selling oranges and lemons to the Forty-Niners. He also pioneered viticulture in California. In addition to table grapes, he was producing fifty thousand gallons of wine a year at his death in 1866. He was well known in Los Angeles and married into the Lugo family. His five brothers all eventually followed him to California. J.W. Wolfskill was the son of William Wolfskill's younger brother Mathius. J.W. Wolfskill built his home near the site of the Los Angeles California Mormon Temple on Santa Monica Boulevard and was also a well-known pioneer of California agriculture. He ranched the property until its sale to Arthur Letts.

Rindge

Frederick Hastings Rindge was born to a wealthy Cambridge, Massachusetts family. His health was never robust, and he left Harvard without graduating. He inherited his parents' fortune while he was still a young man and donated the land for the Cambridge Public Library and a new city hall in their memory. The Rindge name is still well known in Cambridge. He arrived in

California in 1887 and purchased the Rancho Topanga Malibu Sequit from Henry Workman Keller. His initial purchase was for 13,300 acres, but he eventually expanded that to 17,000 acres.

Rindge was active in the fight to make Santa Monica a "no saloon" town, and he personally reimbursed the city for the lost revenue when the measure passed. He was a founder of the Conservative Life Insurance Company (now Pacific Life), was involved with Union Oil Company and had investments in Stockton, San Fernando Valley and Sinaloa, Mexico. His several self-published books waxed poetic about California and his Malibu ranch. He belonged to a number of organizations that mirrored his interests in archaeology, history and religion. One of his projects was the establishment of the First Methodist Episcopal Church of Santa Monica.

Rindge died unexpectedly in 1905 while on a trip to Yreka, leaving his wife, May, to continue his fight to keep the rancho a rural paradise. Ultimately, it fell to his daughter Rhoda May and her husband, Merritt Adamson, to subdivide the property. Adamson was the ranch manager before he married Rindge and started one of the biggest dairy operations in the country, Adohr Farms. The Malibu was one of the last ranchos to be opened to homeowners.

Promoters

The men and women who turned the hills, mesas, beaches and canyons into the West Los Angeles of today listed themselves proudly as "capitalists" on their census forms, in newspaper interviews and in advertising. It was a name they felt described their work, and they were proud of it. It takes vision, skill, entrepreneurship and guts to risk capital on open land twenty-five miles from the center of a small town without much water and develop it into streets, lots, buildings, homes and businesses where people want to live, work and play. The payoff is that today, this land sells for millions of dollars. It takes luck and timing to ride out economic ups and downs; bubbles, panics and depressions; wars; and natural disasters. More than once the promoters ran out of money, but they never lost their enthusiasm for the land they were developing and the communities they were creating. Their vision, their donations of land, streets, parks and other infrastructure to the area shaped it into today's desirable real estate.

Baker

Robert Symington Baker was born in Rhode Island in about 1825 and came to California in 1849 on the steamer *Oregon* as part of the Gold Rush. His firm of Cooke and Baker provided equipment and supplies to the miners, making Baker a wealthy man. He also partnered with General Beale (famous for his part in making California a state) in a large ranching operation in Kern County. They ran cattle and sheep on their Tejon Ranch. (At more than 200,000 acres, it is still the largest privately owned ranch in California.) In 1872, Baker arrived by steamship at the Shoo Fly landing, the rough pier on Santa Monica Bay used to ship "asphaltum" (bitumen) from the tar pits to Northern California, looking for property suitable for raising sheep. His assessment was that the grassy mesa would be perfect for that purpose.

Baker sold his holdings in Kern County to Beale and purchased the Rancho San Vicente y Santa Monica from the Sepulveda heirs. The price was $50,000 for approximately thirty thousand acres. He also bought about two thousand acres of the Rancho Boca de Santa Monica. Baker moved to Los Angeles when he made this purchase. During the next two years, he courted and married Arcadia Bandini de Stearns, the wealthy widow of Don Abel Stearns and the daughter of Juan Bandini, a prominent ranchero with property around San Diego and Riverside.

As the price of wool began to drop, Baker began looking for other ways to use his thirty thousand acres. He approached his former partner, General Beale, about laying out a town called Truxtun (probably a nod to Beale's mother, whose maiden name was Truxtun) as the terminus of the Los Angeles and Truxtun Railroad that would bring goods from Los Angeles to Santa Monica Bay for shipment to San Francisco. General Beale visited the property, but Nevada senator John Percival Jones also visited Los Angeles and became interested in Baker's venture. In 1874, Baker sold three-quarters of the San Vicente y Santa Monica to Senator Jones, who wanted to construct a railroad to his newly opened mines in the Panamint area near Death Valley. Planning began on both the railroad and the town of Santa Monica shortly thereafter. Baker transferred the remainder of his interests in the Rancho y San Vicente de Santa Monica to his wife in 1879 and died in 1894.

Bandini

Arcadia Bandini was born in San Diego in 1827. Her grandfather, Jose Bandini, was in the Spanish navy, fighting at Trafalgar against the British navy as commander of the *Nymphia*, a small supply vessel. Serving in the navy on the coast of South America, he settled in Lima, Peru. Part of his duty was to ferry troops to Alta California to protect the colony. In 1820, he and his son Juan relocated to San Diego. Juan Bandini quickly prospered in San Diego, marrying into the prominent Estudillo family and building a substantial home on the Plaza in San Diego (now the Cosmopolitan Hotel in Old Town, San Diego).

Juan Bandini was at the center of several revolutions against the Mexican government of California and allied himself with the American traders flooding into the colony. In 1841, his oldest daughter, Arcadia, married Don Abel Stearns, one of her father's business partners. Bandini supported the American takeover of California. His wife and daughters sewed the first American flag that flew in San Diego using their petticoats and skirts to create the red, white and blue stars and stripes.

Stearns was forty-three at the time of the marriage, much older than his teenage wife, but the marriage seems to have been a success. (Tiburico Tapia was one of the witnesses for Stearns.) He built a large building on the Plaza in Los Angeles as a commercial building and residence. It was so grand (as opposed to the rest of the city's buildings) that the locals called it "El Palacio." The couple hosted the movers and shakers of Los Angeles in their ballroom—Sepulveda, Machado, Carrillo, Tapia, Wilson, Keller and many others. It was the center of the growing town. Stearns was a very wealthy landowner by 1860, owning Rancho La Habra, Rancho Los Coyotes, Rancho San Juan Cajon de Santa Ana, Rancho Las Bolas, Rancho Jurupa and Rancho La Sierra. When the drought of 1863–64 wiped out the cattle industry, Stearns was overextended and land poor. However, he recovered his footing and was a wealthy man when he died suddenly in 1871.

Arcadia found herself a wealthy young widow in Los Angeles. R.S. Baker moved to Los Angeles in 1872 to manage his new venture—Rancho San Vicente y Santa Monica. Only a year older than Arcadia and a widower, they must have been thrown together often in the Los Angeles social scene. They married in 1875, uniting two of the largest fortunes in California. Baker tore down the "Palacio" and built the even more luxurious Baker Block. Arcadia furnished it with Aubusson carpets, antiques and elegant china. Baker also built a home on Ocean Avenue in his new town of Santa Monica, where Arcadia spent summers and her last few years. She did not have children of her own but was always accompanied by a bevy of nieces and nephews contributed by her numerous siblings. Her brother Juan Bandini married Esperanza Sepulveda, the granddaughter of Francisco

Arcadia Bandini de Baker was the leader of Los Angeles society from the time of her marriage to Don Abel Stearns at age fourteen until her death in Santa Monica in 1912. After Stearns's death in 1871, she married Robert Symington Baker.

Sepulveda, the original owner of the Rancho San Vicente y Santa Monica, producing two of Arcadia's nieces.

Baker transferred Rancho San Vicente y Santa Monica to Arcadia in 1879, making her partners with Senator Jones in the development of Santa Monica and the surrounding land. They formed the Santa Monica Land & Water Company in 1897 to manage their joint interests. Over the years, she contributed her name to numerous projects—Arcadia Street in Los Angeles and in Santa Monica and the Arcadia Hotel, once the most elegant hotel on the coast. She also donated land to improve her community—the Home for Disabled Volunteer Soldiers (today's VA West Los Angeles Medical Center in Westwood). Palisades Park in Santa Monica, Woodlawn Cemetery in Santa Monica, Lincoln Park (now Christine E. Reed Park), numerous right of ways for trolleys and roads and the original site of the Santa Monica Bay Women's Club, to name just a few. At her death in 1912 she was considered the wealthiest woman in the state of California. Since she died without a will, her numerous heirs spent many years in court arguing over the division of her estate.

Jones

John Percival Jones was born in England in 1829 and immigrated with his parents to the United States as a baby. He grew up in Ohio among thirteen siblings and started a career in banking when he finished high school. However, the discovery of gold made banking seem tame, and in 1849, he and a brother set off for the gold fields of California. Fittingly, he sailed from Cleveland on a small ship named *Eureka*. It was a long and eventful trip that ended with Jones and the other passengers being tried for mutiny in San Francisco.

After talking himself out of that dilemma, he began his search for gold. His mining activities took him to Tuolumne, Calaveras and Trinity Counties in the hills of Northern California over a twenty-year period. He was a familiar sight in the mining camps and was well known to the players of his day. His rescue of several miners in the Yellow Jacket mine fire made him famous and respected in the gold fields. He was elected sheriff of Trinity County and also represented the area in the state senate. In 1867, he ran for lieutenant governor of California but lost the election.

Giving up politics with this defeat, Jones moved to Gold Hill, near Virginia City in Nevada, to try his hand at finding gold in the Comstock area. Jones found, against all odds, a huge deposit of silver in the Crown Point mine. The find was estimated at a value of $600 million. Jones suddenly was one of the wealthiest men in the West. With his finances secure, Jones returned to politics. He was elected as a Republican to the United States Senate from Nevada in 1872. He served in that position for thirty years until his retirement in 1903. In Washington, he championed Free Silver and also Asian Exclusion bills.

Senator John Percival Jones served the State of Nevada as a senator for thirty years but spent much of his time and energy promoting Santa Monica. *Courtesy of the Santa Monica Public Library Image Archives.*

In 1875, Senator Jones was bitten by the railroad bug and invested some of his newfound wealth with R.S. Baker in a scheme to create a railroad link to the Panamint mines near Death Valley. Jones and Baker created the city of Santa Monica as a terminus for their railroad. He was a founding partner with Arcadia Bandini de Stearns de Baker of the Santa Monica Land & Water Company, selling all his stock to Robert Conran Gillis around 1902. Senator Jones built his beautiful mansion on Ocean Avenue and named it

Miramar—a name that continues today as the name of the hotel built on the same site. Senator Jones's wife, Georgina, lived at Miramar along with their three daughters and often without Senator Jones, who traveled extensively, though he retired there after his service in Washington.

His brother Robert Jones, his nephew Harry M. Gorham and his son Roy Jones were all eventually involved in the business of developing Santa Monica, and they all lived in the city. They all owned stock in the Santa Monica Land & Water Company and were part of its development projects for many years.

Vawter

William D. Vawter (left) opened Santa Monica's first retail store and, with his sons, became one of Santa Monica's leading families. Dr. Charles Lindsey is standing beside Vawter.

Williamson Dunn Vawter was born in Vernon, Indiana, and immigrated to California in 1875. He was a member of the Indiana Colony and purchased a ranch in the area that eventually became Pasadena's business area. Attracted by the possibilities (and glowing advertising) for the Santa Monica area, he and his sons relocated there and opened a general store. The store was followed by a lumberyard and a planing mill. Along with his sons, he obtained the first franchise for a streetcar line and built a five-mile extension from Santa Monica to the Old Soldiers Home. He founded the First National Bank of Santa Monica in a brick building that he built in 1886 at the corner of Third Street and Oregon Avenue.

Vawter's son William S. Vawter was also born in Vernon, Indiana, and immigrated to California with his father in 1875. He was involved in both the bank and the streetcar operations. He built one of the first houses in South Santa Monica (Ocean

Park). Another son, Edwin James Vawter, was involved with his father and brother in the bank and the streetcar business. He also planted a number of acres in South Santa Monica in carnations, creating a profitable industry for early Santa Monica.

Sherman

Moses Hazeltine Sherman started his career as a teacher in Arizona. He was the first school principal in Prescott, Arizona, and was appointed adjutant general of the territory. He preferred to be called General Sherman for the rest of his career. With his brother-in-law Eli P. Clark (he was married to Sherman's sister Lucy), Sherman created a successful business in Prescott. They also developed a railroad that ran from Prescott to Seligman. Finding out that sand and water were damaging the steam engines used for the

General Sherman enjoyed putting together impromptu outings to the beach or to Mount Lowe. He would stop his private trolley car, the Mermaid, along San Vicente Boulevard and pick up wives and children of his friends for these excursions. This photo was taken on a beach outing.

cable car effort in Los Angeles, Sherman and Clark went to Los Angeles to introduce the electric trolleys that were successful in New York City. The electric trolleys were cheaper to build and operate. In Los Angeles, Sherman and Clark purchased several short lines and created the Los Angeles Consolidated Railway and the first interurban railway—the Pasadena and Los Angeles Electric Railway. They then went on to create the trolley lines that connected Santa Monica, Sawtelle, Westgate, Ocean Park, Playa del Rey and many other suburbs to Los Angeles.

Sherman was an enthusiastic man, and at six feet nine inches, he stood out in every crowd. He would often show up unannounced at the R.C. Gillis home on Adelaide Drive while the family was still in bed and would order breakfast from their Chinese cook. He would then pick up everyone who lived on San Vicente Boulevard for excursions around Los Angeles on his private trolley car, the Mermaid. His wife and children lived in San Francisco most of the time, and when the 1906 San Francisco earthquake hit, he was in Los Angeles. He and a group of volunteers put medical supplies and other assistance on a train and took it north to help the city. It was the first relief train to reach San Francisco.

Sherman and Clark remained friends and business partners their entire lives, and both died in 1932. They are buried with their wives under a double stone at Forest Lawn in Los Angeles.

Gillis

William Templeton Gillis was a pharmacist who moved to Santa Monica from Nova Scotia in 1887, opening up a drugstore. His brother, Robert Conran Gillis, also a pharmacist, visited him shortly after he arrived in Santa Monica. He met his future wife, Frances Lindsey from Norridgewok, Maine, over a corn popper—he had never seen popcorn done in a fireplace before. Frances was the daughter of Congressman Stephen Decatur Lindsay. Her father was a leading Maine politician and abolitionist who was instrumental in Lincoln's nomination. He represented Maine's Third District from 1877 to 1883. William Edward Sawtelle, the banker who gave his name to Sawtelle, was a relative by marriage. One of her brothers was a dentist, and one was a doctor, both practicing in Santa Monica. Both Gillis brothers began developing real estate soon after they arrived in Santa Monica, although W.T. Gillis stayed in the pharmacy business both in Santa Monica and in Redlands until his death.

W.T. Gillis developed several tracts in Sawtelle. R.C. Gillis began buying the stock of the Santa Monica Land & Water Company in about 1900 as part of a group of investors that included Roy Jones, Henry M. Gorham and Charles LeRoy Bundy. At this time, the company owned about twenty thousand acres of land—the Rancho San Vicente y Santa Monica and some of the Rancho Boca de Santa Monica. While at various points Gillis sold stock to other investors—General Sherman, Arthur H. Fleming and Alphonzo Bell to name a few—and deeded land to other corporations, he remained head of and held the controlling interest in the Santa Monica Land & Water Company for the rest of his life. Over the years, he purchased more acreage from the Marquez heirs and from others who had purchased pieces of the Rancho Boca de Santa Monica.

This photo of Robert C. Gillis was taken about the time he purchased the Santa Monica Land & Water Company. A native of Nova Scotia, he became a naturalized citizen and was a major promoter of both Los Angeles and Santa Monica.

In 1909, W.T. Gillis succumbed to the consumption that apparently brought him to California. R.C. Gillis went on to develop numerous neighborhoods that are now some of the most desirable residential areas of West Los Angeles—the Palisades, Brentwood and Pacific Palisades. He also owned the *Santa Monica Outlook* for a number of years and was involved in numerous other business ventures during his long career. Among his many gifts of land were the right of way down San Vicente Boulevard, a large donation to Troop Polytechnic Institute (now California Institute of Technology) and the land at the northern end of the bluff that completed Palisades Park. He was part of the consortium that built the San Diego and Eastern Railway and was active with the Southern Pacific for a number of years. He died in 1947.

Fleming

Arthur Henry Fleming was born in Ontario, Canada. An attorney by profession, he switched to the timber business when he came to California in 1896. He was married to Clara Fowler, a niece of Cyrus McCormick—the inventor of the McCormick Reaper and one of the wealthiest men in the country. Her father, Eldridge Merick Fowler, was an investor in the Madera Sugar Pine Company in the Fresno area. Both Clara and her father died within weeks of each other in 1904. These early and untimely deaths left Fleming with a small daughter and as trustee of his wife's fortune. He often invested money with R.C. Gillis and General Sherman. One of his first investments was the Beach Land Company and Playa del Rey. In the lumber business, he was known for the Madera Lumber Company, the Minerets and Western Railroad and the Sugar Pine Lumber Company all located near Fresno. R.C. Gillis invested money with him in the Sugar Pine Lumber Company and other lumbering ventures.

He made his home in Pasadena and was very active in the founding of Troop Polytechnic Institute. He made a $5 million donation to the university in the name of his late wife and also donated twenty-two acres of land to the campus. Dr. Robert A. Millikan credited him with carrying the institute through its "teething" stages by assuming its deficits during its early years. He espoused Andrew Carnegie's philosophy about wealth and felt that creating the institute was his way to use his wealth as a force for good.

Bundy

Nathan Pearl Bundy was an early settler in Santa Monica, arriving from Ames, Iowa, at the Shoo Fly Pier via San Francisco in 1876. (The family celebrated their arrival annually with a picnic at Inspiration Point for many years.) He opened a dry goods store and was a prominent business owner in Santa Monica. He lived in Santa Monica before moving to Westgate in his later years. Among his major achievements were the five sons who followed him into business in West Los Angeles. His youngest child was daughter Sara Elizabeth Bundy.

Francis Eugene Bundy was first a jeweler and then went into the oil business. Using the proceeds from that business, he bought tracts of land in Santa Monica to subdivide and sell. He was involved in the East Ocean Park and Sierra Vista tracts, as well as in developing commercial real estate. His first building was the F.E. Bundy Block on Third Street. One of the commercial buildings he built still stands on West Channel Road in Santa

Monica Canyon. He built and sold over five hundred homes and buildings during his career.

George Guy Bundy first owned the livery stable used by many Santa Monica residents; the Gillis family kept their horses there until they built their own stable. Once automobiles took over, he owned the Studebaker dealership and was very active in Santa Monica affairs. He also raised horses and sold many of them to the movie studios for use in Westerns.

Charles LeRoy Bundy went into real estate development after spending ten years in banking. He was an executive with the Santa Monica Land & Water Company and worked on the Westgate subdivision and numerous other tracts. He married Harriet Bernice (Hallie) Loomis, the daughter of Lawrence Duncan Loomis, another Santa Monica real estate man.

Thomas Clark Bundy was a champion tennis player, finishing runner-up in the U.S. National Championship men's singles in 1910 and winning the doubles in 1912, 1913 and 1914. He married May Sutton, who won both the U.S. National Championship and Wimbledon Championship in 1905. She was the first American and the first non-Brit to win the singles title. T.C. Bundy went on to develop land in Sherman Oaks and started the Los Angeles Tennis Club. (Their daughter Dorothy Bundy Cheney won the 1938 Australian Championship in 1938 and is still playing tennis in her nineties in San Diego.)

Nathan Pearl Bundy Jr. was a promising Los Angeles lawyer, but he died suddenly at the age of forty-one of ptomaine poisoning. Recently married, he was in San Francisco at the time to accept an important post with the Southern Pacific Legal Department.

Sara (Sadie) Bundy was a teacher and administrator in the Los Angeles schools for a number of years, serving as the principal of Louis Pasteur Junior High School for many years.

Kinney

Abbot Kinney was well traveled both as a young man and during his career as a tobacco broker. He had seen most of Europe, India, Australia and Hawaii when he first came to California in 1880. Delayed by a snowstorm in San Francisco, he made a side trip to Southern California. While there, he discovered that his asthma improved dramatically. Like so many other respiratory disease sufferers, he immediately decided to move to Los Angeles. He first settled near Sierra Madre on a ranch he named Kinneloa. However, he and his wife found summers there too warm and built a summer home in Santa Monica in 1887.

Abbot Kinney's energetic, enthusiastic personality was a major influence on West Los Angeles through his development of Ocean Park and Venice Beach. *Courtesy of Security Pacific Collection/Los Angeles Public Library.*

Kinney had many interests, including conservation and forestry. He was appointed chairman of the California Board of Forestry. One of his accomplishments was an agency designed to prevent forest fires and follow-on flooding in the San Gabriel Mountains. In 1887, he established the first forestry station in Rustic Canyon on land donated by Jones and Baker. There he planted twenty species of eucalyptus trees in order to study how they adapted to the California coastal climate.

He was also very interested in the plight of the American Indian. In 1873, prior to his California adventures, he joined a U.S. Geological Survey team that was mapping Sioux reservations. In 1883, he—in his capacity as U.S. Indian agent—and activist Helen Hunt Jackson, author of the popular novel *Ramona*, wrote a report on the plight of the California Mission Indians.

As part of his involvement with Santa Monica, Kinney bought two pieces of land. One was on the bluff above the beach north of Santa Monica above the Long Wharf (now Huntington Palisades), and one from W.D. Vawter was on the beach south of the new town. He also built a house on Ocean Avenue. His intention for the land on the bluff was to create a resort above the wharf. When that project did not work out, he turned his attention to the other piece and eventually developed both Ocean Park and Venice.

Loomis

Edward LeRoy Loomis moved his family from McPherson, Kansas, where he was the deputy county clerk, to Southern California in 1886. He was one of the founders of the company that became the Title Insurance and Trust Company of Los Angeles. He and his wife both seem to have died young (she was thirty-seven, and he was forty-two), so their immigration to California was probably influenced by their health. They lived on an orange grove in Duarte before moving to the Los Angeles area. Their three children, Lawrence Duncan, Melville LeRoy and Harriet Bernice (Hallie), all remained in the West Los Angeles area. Roy was educated at the University of Southern California and became a doctor. In 1908, he took over as superintendent of a new hospital in Santa Monica. Hallie married C.L. Bundy and lived in Santa Monica and Westgate.

L.D. Loomis went into real estate sales in Santa Monica. His name shows up as a stockholder and as manager of the Pacific Land Company in 1904. That company was active in developing Sawtelle. He also was part of the firm of Heath, Loomis & Cole with offices in Sawtelle and Ocean Park. The company was a selling agent for the Santa Monica Land & Water Company.

Lawrence Duncan Loomis was active in the development of Westgate and sold real estate in Santa Monica Canyon and Ocean Park.

He was part of the development team for the first Westgate tract along with his brother-in-law C.L. Bundy. He also developed and sold properties in Santa Monica Canyon along Mabery and Channel Roads. He was the sales agent for Gillette's Regent Square. He and Bundy lived next door to each other on San Vicente Boulevard in Westgate for many years.

His son, Arthur Lawrence Loomis, was born at the corner of Wilshire Boulevard and Third Street. He was a star athlete at Santa Monica High School, lettering in football and baseball. It was a cause célèbre in Santa Monica and Los Angeles when he eloped with Ynez Ward, Arcadia Bandini de Stearns de Baker's grandniece, at age seventeen. The marriage ended in divorce in 1932, and Arthur subsequently married Dorothy Gillis, daughter of R.C. Gillis. Arthur Loomis was a stockbroker and was active in real estate, serving as president of the Santa Monica Land & Water Company from his father-in-law's death in 1948 until his own death in 1979. He also served as head of the Pacific Palisades Chamber of Commerce and president of the Greater Los Angeles Realty Board, worked on Alphonzo Bell Jr.'s congressional campaigns and was active in persuading Ronald Reagan to run for governor of California.

Bell

Alphonzo Edward Bell was born in Los Angeles to a family that was already distinguished for its contributions to the growing city. His father, James George Bell, owned the Bell Station Ranch (now the City of Bell) near Santa Fe Springs. His mother was the daughter of Susan Hollenbeck—her uncle, Ed Hollenbeck, founded the First National Bank and developed parts of East Los Angeles. Since his parents were devout Presbyterians, Alphonzo "Phonzie" Bell was brought up in a family that prized integrity and strict morality. His father also liked tennis and built a tennis court near their home. Bell attended Occidental College (founded by his father) and distinguished himself in several sports but was particularly well known for his tennis game. He won silver and bronze medals at the 1904 Olympics held in St. Louis, Missouri. He continued to play tennis all his life with other California players, including T.C. Bundy.

After Occidental, Bell studied for the ministry but left after two years, apparently finding that public speaking was not his forte. He met his wife, Minnewa, on the tennis courts when she was visiting friends in Los Angeles. She had as strong a religious background as he did and was also interested in art and landscaping. They set up their first home at Bell Station. He purchased land around Bell and also in Santa Fe Springs. Bell persuaded Union Oil Company to drill for oil on his Santa Fe Springs property. The well was a gusher, and Bell's land turned out to be one of the largest oil fields in California, making him a wealthy man.

After one of the wells on his property burned, endangering his family, he moved his wife and children to Jake Danzinger's ranch near Beverly Hills. Bell's background meant that he felt great responsibility for his newfound wealth, and he wanted to use it well. This idea colored all of his real estate projects—he felt that he had a responsibility to develop communities that would be the finest residential areas in the country. Bel-Air Estates, the Riviera, Mandeville, Castellammare, the Bel-Air Country Club and the Bel-Air Bay Club are all tributes to his values (and his interest in Italian hill towns). His strong views on alcohol were well known, and he did not allow liquor to be served in his clubs during Prohibition. He also had strong views on the decadence of the movie industry and did not want to sell property to anyone involved.

Bell lived until 1947. He is remembered for his many contributions to Occidental College, the University of California at Los Angeles (UCLA) and the Los Angeles Presbyterian Church. His son Alphonzo E. Bell Jr. represented West Los Angeles in Congress for sixteen years.

Garbutt

Francis (Frank) Clarkson Garbutt was born in 1837 in Canada and lived in Missouri, Illinois and Massachusetts and struck gold in Colorado before he settled in Los Angeles. He served in the Union army during the Civil War, encouraged his outspoken wife in her political activities and started a dynasty of "Franks."

His son, Francis (Frank) Alderman Garbutt, was born in 1869 in Mason City, Illinois, and came to California with his father. He was a founder of Union Oil, and he invented many oil drilling tools. He also founded Paramount Pictures and invested in the aviation company that became Lockheed Martin. However, it was his enthusiasm for amateur sports that helped him put his mark on Los Angeles. He was a founder of the Los Angeles Athletic Club and worked with A. Bell to create the Riviera Country Club. He was an early investor in Playa del Rey along with R.C. Gillis. He also raced fast cars and was influential in bringing the 1932 Olympics to Los Angeles. He owned the inter-island ferry company that ran between Terminal Island and San Pedro. He also designed, built and raced yachts.

His other projects included the California Yacht Club, the Hollywood Athletic Club, the Santa Monica Athletic Club, Surf & Sand Club, Pacific Coast Club and the Deauville Beach Club. His daughter Melonie married Frank Hathaway. The Hathaway family continues to be involved in the Los Angeles Athletic Club and the California Yacht Club. His son was Francis (Frank) E. Garbutt.

Huntington

Collis Potter Huntington was one of the Big Four—the four California capitalists who built the Central Pacific Railroad that connected the East and West Coasts in 1869. Along with Leland Stanford, Charles Crocker and Mark Hopkins, as well as R.S. Baker (who was not part of the Big Four, though he made his money the same way), Huntington began his career in California selling goods to the Forty-Niners. The group also established the Southern Pacific (SP) Railroad that connected Los Angeles to the East. C.P. Huntington wanted the terminus of the Southern Pacific's line and the Port of Los Angeles to be built at the foot of Potrero Canyon just north of Santa Monica. A long struggle ensued between his chosen site and San Pedro, which also wanted to be the Port of Los Angeles. In 1893, Huntington built the Long Wharf at the end of the Southern Pacific tracks in Santa Monica, and for some years, freight was shipped from there to the rest of the world. As part of his plan, Huntington bought the land on the bluff above the wharf from Abbot Kinney with the intention of creating a mansion above his port. However, San Pedro won the honor of being the Port of Los Angeles after a bitter political battle, and the house was never built.

C.P. Huntington's nephew Henry Edwards Huntington married his uncle's widow, Arabella, and they sold the land on the bluff to the Pacific Palisades Association after Huntington's death. It was ultimately developed into the Huntington Palisades. Following in his uncle's footsteps, H.E. Huntington purchased the Los Angeles Railway (the Yellow Car system) and then developed the Pacific Electric system (Red Car system). The Red Cars connected the far-flung real estate of Southern California and made it possible for residents to purchase homes in the outlying regions and still work in the core.

The trolley system had over twenty streetcar lines and 1,250 trolleys at its height. It was possible to go from San Vicente Boulevard in Santa Monica to Pomona and Mount Lowe and everything in between. Huntington shared ownership of the Red Cars with the Southern Pacific until 1911 when he sold his interest to the SP. He retained control of the Los Angeles Railway until his death. H.E. Huntington built his home in San Marino, and at his death, the property became the Huntington Library, Art Collections and Botanical Gardens. There are a number of streets and communities in Southern California named for the family.

Scott

Charles Holmes Scott graduated from the University of Southern California and was ordained a Methodist minister in 1905. He came to California as a child of six from Michigan. He ministered to congregations in Ventura, Pasadena, San Bernadino, Ontario and Glendale before Bishop Adna W. Leonard asked him to find a permanent location for the Southern Californian Chautauqua movement. Scott began searching for the best location in 1921 and making the contacts he would need to put together the real estate deal. Scott formed the Pacific Palisades Association along with a number of prominent businessmen—R.C. Gillis, Albert Joseph Wallace, Walter L. Armacost, Charles Clarke Chapman and Andrew M. Chaffey. Scott shaped and influenced the development of the Pacific Palisades until the early 1930s, when the financial crash forced changes in the way the association was organized. At that time, Scott left the organization and joined the Santa Monica Land & Water Company as a sales agent. He was successful in this endeavor and raised his six children in the Santa Monica and Los Angeles area. He died in 1952.

Letts/Janss

Arthur Letts was born in Holmby, England, in 1862. After receiving his education and completing an apprenticeship in the dry goods business, he immigrated to Canada. He worked in the dry goods business in Toronto for several years and also served in the Canadian army. He migrated to Seattle in the early 1890s, only to have the store he was working in destroyed by fire three days after he started work. Undaunted, he scrambled together some goods and opened his own store in a tent. Apparently not satisfied with Seattle as a site for his business, he arrived in Los Angeles in 1896. As luck would have it, a dry goods firm had recently gone bankrupt at Fourth and Broadway. He was able to assume the lease and purchase their goods cheaply. That was the beginning of the Broadway Department Stores. His new venture was damaged by fire at the end of the first week, but Letts persevered, and the store prospered to become one of the largest chains on the West Coast. He was also a major investor in the Bullocks chain of stores.

Letts was interested in education and served as a trustee of the State Normal School (which eventually became UCLA). His main hobby was gardening, and he surrounded his home in Hollywood with a garden of rare plants and trees. The garden was open to the public and was a stop on the Red Car route. After his death, the garden was demolished and the estate subdivided. Some of the specimen cacti were purchased by Henry Huntington and are now part of the Huntington Desert Garden at the Huntington Library.

He purchased part of the Wolfskill Ranch in 1919, intending to develop it into a mixed-use community of retail and homes. He also envisioned a university for his new town. His untimely death in 1923 left the development's completion to his son-in-law Harold Janss and the Janss Investment Company. Janss was married to Letts's daughter Gladys and was a partner with his brother James in the Janss Investment Company. The Janss brothers had already made a success of their developments in the San Fernando Valley and had the experience needed to develop the Wolfskill property. They started selling lots in Westwood in 1922. Janss developed both Westwood Village and Holmby Hills. He was also involved in the move of the State Normal School to the Westwood area and the establishment of UCLA.

Chapter 2 LANDSCAPE

A satellite passing over West Los Angeles today peers down on a bustling suburb—streets, houses, apartments, high-rises, trees, people, commercial districts, parks, beaches and automobiles. A satellite passing over the same area in 1542 would have seen open land, mesas, mountains, streams and trees. That is what Juan Rodriquez Cabrillo saw when he anchored his ships in Santa Monica Bay that year. The satellite would have no doubt seen Indian villages as well, located near the base of the hills and close to water sources. Subsequent satellite passes would not have marked much change for roughly the next three hundred years.

The Chumash lived in the coastal areas. The Tongva Indians' village was near the Kuruvungna Springs (now University High School in West Los Angeles). Grinding stones and burned ground testify to their use of the land and its abundant resources of water, game, fish and acorns.

In 1765, the Portola expedition, searching for a passage to Northern California through the mountains, camped near the springs. The expedition's description of the area was similar to what Cabrillo saw.

However, things were about to change.

Ranchos

The Spanish/Mexican legal system assumed that the king (or the Mexican government after the revolution succeeded in 1821) owned all of the land discovered by its explorers. As part of the colonial process, the king granted concessions of land to individuals as rewards for services rendered. Land concessions for ranchos were used extensively in Alta California to ensure settlement of its open lands and to hold it for Spain/Mexico. This custom dictated much of how the area developed during its first hundred years. The names and contours of the original ranchos survive as a lasting legacy of the origins of California.

Under both Spanish and Mexican rule, five land grants were made to various individuals for the rolling mesas and hills that now make up West Los Angeles. Approximately sixty-eight thousand acres of land were handed out using this system. After the revolution, the Mexican government required the grantees to build homes and use their acres for farming and ranching as part of ownership requirements. Soon the hills and mesas were dotted with adobes, horses and cattle. All five of the ranchos developed unique characteristics based on their geography and their individual owners.

Rancho Topanga Malibu Sequit

Jose Bartoleme Tapia was granted the Rancho Topanga Malibu Sequit in 1804 as a reward for his army service. His 13,315.70 acres were located between the mountains and Pacific Ocean and today are known as Malibu and Topanga Canyon. Its canyons and isolation also made it a perfect hideout for smugglers and horse thieves. The newspapers of the day report numerous arrests and trials of criminals found in the area.

Rancho La Ballona

Rancho La Ballona was granted to the Augustin Machado and Felipe Talamantes families in 1821. Today Marina del Rey, Venice Mar Vista, Palms and some of Culver City are located on this 13,919.90 acres.

Rancho San Vicente y Santa Monica

The San Vicente was granted to Francisco Sepulveda, along with a pasture called Santa Monica, by Governor Juan Alvarado in 1839. His 30,259.65 acres was the largest of the five grants and today encompasses Santa Monica, Brentwood and the western edge of Bel-Air.

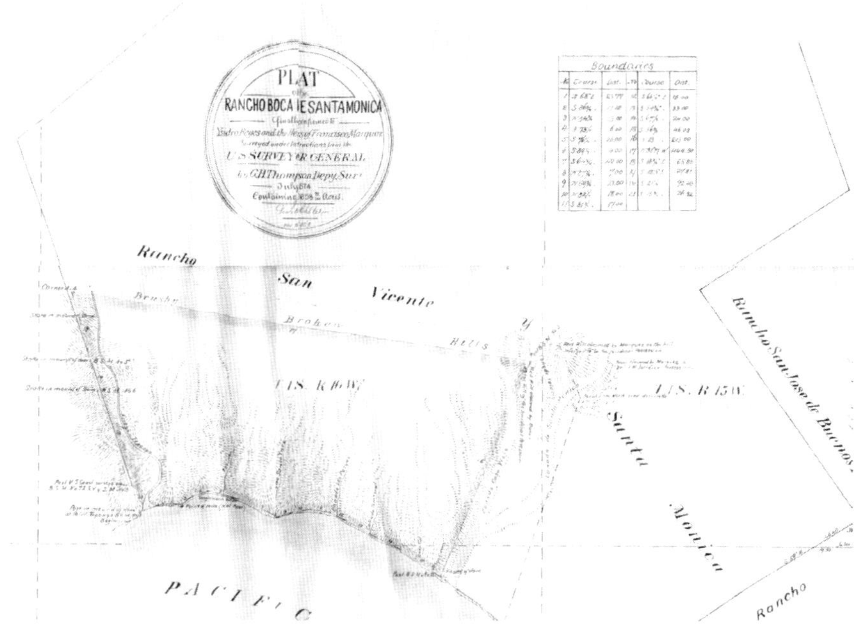

This surveyor's map was one of the documents submitted to the court as part of the settlement of the boundary dispute between the Sepulveda and the Reyes Marquez families. The dotted line between the two grants is the disputed territory. This is the map submitted to the Marquez heirs.

Rancho Boca de Santa Monica

The Boca de Santa Monica was granted to Yisdro Reyes and Francisco Marquez in 1839 as well. Today, their 6,656 acres is Pacific Palisades and Santa Monica Canyon. In the 1860s, Angelenos began to travel to the mouth of Santa Monica Canyon to camp along the creeks and trees as an escape from the summer heat. In the 1880s, the Marquez family created a bathhouse at the mouth of Santa Monica Canyon.

Rancho San Jose Buenos Ayres

Bel-Air, UCLA, Westwood and Holmby Hills are located on the 4,438.69 acres given to Maximo Alanis in 1843 and called Rancho San Jose Buenos Ayres.

The boundaries of these properties were delineated by a vaquero riding from a stake placed in the ground to the length of a fifty-foot *reata* (leather braided rope or lasso), setting another stake and repeating the process. Landmarks were streams, rocks, trees or other distinguishing formations. The diseños or maps that document the grants are reminiscent of a child's sketch.

Rancho life was based around the herds of cattle and horses that roamed the hills and mesas. Hides and tallow were the primary products generated from the great herds of cattle. With little cash money available, barter was the basis for the economy. Hides were often used as currency for paying bills and debts. Compound interest was unheard of. The hospitality of the ranchos was legendary—guests often stayed for weeks on the far-flung properties. The grazing lands were not fenced. If someone needed to butcher a cow for food, they left the hide in a prominent place for its owner to find and ate their fill. No one pursued them for theft. There were few lawyers in the territory, and disputes were usually settled peaceably among friends.

This pleasant life began to change with the American takeover of California. Prior to 1845, American settlers had drifted into California as trappers and traders. Some stayed to make their homes there, often marrying into the Californio families, converting to Catholicism and becoming Mexican citizens. The Bear Flag Revolt fomented by American settlers in Sonoma and abetted by Fremont and his troops followed the start of the Mexican American War in 1846. The Treaty of Hidalgo ended the war and ceded Alta California, Arizona and New Mexico to the Americans. The Californios had been on both sides of the struggle, and they were no doubt grateful that the treaty recognized and protected their land grants.

The Gold Rush in 1849 meant new and very profitable markets for cattle. The Californios drove huge herds north to feed the miners and the others in the gold fields. For the first time, the rancheros were making real hard money. The new funds fueled an extravagant lifestyle of match races, fiestas and silver saddles. Competition from cattle driven from other states dropped prices at the end of the 1850s, and the Californios found themselves unable to maintain their lifestyles. Many borrowed money at exorbitant and compounding interest rates.

In addition, once statehood was granted in 1850, American law was applied to the new state. Congress passed the Land Act in 1851 providing for three commissioners to "ascertain and settle the Private Land Claims in California." The Land Act required that all titles to Spanish and Mexican grants be submitted to the commission in order to validate ownership. The goal of this process was to settle boundary disputes and handle squatter claims. The Californios quickly discovered that their flexible boundaries and informal record keeping were a handicap in these detailed legal proceedings. In order to defend their land, they incurred large legal fees, debts and more mortgages that often forced the sale of their properties.

By 1851, the Rancho Topanga Malibu Sequit had passed into the hands of Leon Victor Prudhomme (a grandson-in-law of Jose Tapia). Prudhomme discovered when he filed his claim that the title was not sufficiently documented, and his claim was denied. In 1857, he sold the land to Mathew Keller, who managed to obtain a patent in 1872.

The titles to the Rancho San Vicente y Santa Monica and the Rancho Boca de Santa Monica were complicated by a boundary dispute between the Sepulveda and Marquez families over competing claims to land at the mouth of Santa Monica Canyon. The case dragged on, and in 1872, the Sepulveda heirs sold the land to R.S. Baker for $55,000. Ultimately the dispute was settled, and the patent was issued in 1881. The Rancho Boca de Santa Monica's patent was issued in 1882.

The Rancho San Jose de Buenos Ayres was sold to Benjamin D. Wilson, known as "Don Benito," and W.T.B. Sanford in 1858, and they received the patent in 1866. The rancho was sold again to John W. Wolfskill in 1884. The Rancho La Ballona was patented to its original owners in 1873. However, Benjamin D. Wilson had already foreclosed on a fourth of the land for a

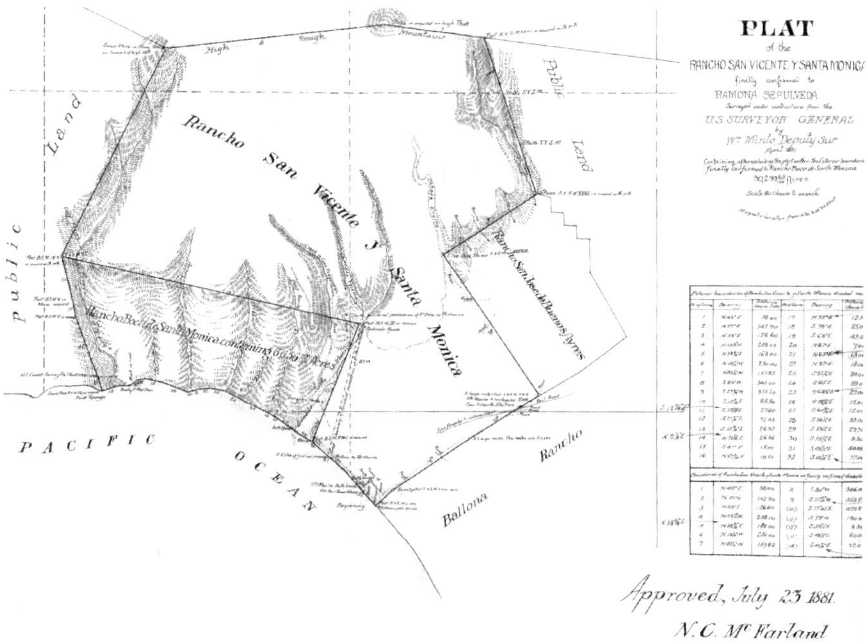

This map was submitted to the Sepulveda heirs as part of the settlement with the Reyes/ Marquez heirs. It also shows the relationship between the Rancho Ballona and Rancho Buenos Ayres.

loan made in 1854. Wilson in turn sold his interest to George Sanford and John D. Young.

By the 1870s, the pastoral era of West Los Angeles was passing and the next act was about to begin—the subdivision of the land into neighborhoods and communities.

Subdivisions

Santa Monica

Asphalt sellers and beachgoers were the first groups to find and use the Santa Monica area for something other than cattle herds. Asphalt from the La Brea Tar Pits was moved by wagon to the Shoo Fly Pier at the base of the arroyo on the Rancho San Vicente y Santa Monica to be loaded on ships for San Francisco. In the 1860s, Dr. A.B. Hayward pitched his family's camp tent in the mouth of Santa Monica Canyon on the Rancho Boca de Santa Monica, moving there to avoid the dust and heat of summer in Los Angeles. Other families joined him, leasing campsites from the Marquez family, and the Rancho Boca de Santa Monica became a popular summer destination. Soon there was a small grocery store, a huge sleeping tent and a small store for sundries to serve the campers' needs.

The price of wool soared during and after the Civil War. In the early 1870s, the price had risen from twelve cents to around forty-five cents a pound. Something of a bubble developed, and California landowners hastened to add and expand sheep herds on their lands. R.S. Baker was already raising sheep on his lands in Kern County and purchased the Rancho San Vicente y Santa Monica to further expand his herds. (R.S. Baker was not the founder of Bakersfield, contrary to some sources. That honor belongs to Colonel Thomas Baker.) Alas, the price of wool dropped back to its more normal pricing in 1873, bursting the bubble. In 1874, Baker sold two-thirds of the Rancho San Vicente to Senator John Percival Jones of Nevada. The two men had ambitious plans to create a railroad that would compete with the Southern Pacific and turn Santa Monica Bay into the port for Los Angeles.

The railroad was needed to bring Jones's silver ore from the Panamint area near Inyo to Santa Monica Bay for transport to smelters located in Northern California. The railroad would replace the mule teams used at the time and circumvent the Southern Pacific's goal of monopolizing the freight business. The Los Angeles and Independence Railroad was built in 1875

An early photo of Santa Monica. The trees defined what would become Ocean Avenue. The Southern Pacific train was parked in the arroyo. The fast-growing town already had homes along Ocean Avenue and a church.

from downtown Los Angeles to a wharf in Santa Monica. The Panamint mines played out fairly quickly, and the line was never extended beyond downtown Los Angeles. It was never successful financially and was sold to the Southern Pacific in 1877.

As part of their port plans, Jones and Baker laid out a new town at the terminus of their railroad. They named their new town Santa Monica after the springs located on their property. The tidy grid of streets was designed with the avenues named after states—Nevada Avenue (now Wilshire Boulevard) was the center of the town—and numbered streets. The first sale of lots was widely advertised, and many Los Angeles residents made the trek to the beach to participate in the auction. Two steamboats loaded with eager buyers came down from San Francisco. The price for a lot started at seventy-five dollars. On July 15, 1875, the keynote speaker, the Honorable Thomas Fitch, known as the "silver tongued orator of the Pacific," gave a stirring sales pitch for the new community:

> *On Wednesday afternoon at one o'clock we will sell at public outcry to the highest bidder; the Pacific Ocean, draped with a Western sky of scarlet*

> *and gold; we will sell a bay filled with white-winged ships. We will sell a southern horizon rimmed with a choice collection of purple mountains, carved in castles and turrets and domes. We will sell a frostless, bracing, warm yet unlanquid air, braided in and out with sunshine and adorned with the breath of flowers. The purchaser of this job lot of climate and scenery will be presented with a deed to a piece of land. The title to the land will be guaranteed by the present owner. The title to the ocean and the sunset, the hills, and the clouds, the breath of the life giving ozone, and the song of the birds is guaranteed by the beneficent God who bestowed them in all their beauty and thereto by almightier warrant as an incorruptible hereditament to run with the land forever.*

Fitch's oratory swayed his listeners to purchase more than $85,000 worth of lots during the two days of the auction. The first lot at the corner of Utah and Ocean Avenues went for $500, while lots farther back from the ocean went for $75. The new owners began to build houses, streets and businesses on the mesa overlooking the ocean and beaches, bringing Jones and Baker's city to life. Twenty-one buildings were completed by the end of July

The National Home for Disabled Volunteer Soldiers

Santa Monica continued to grow at a good pace thanks to the railroad line from Los Angeles, which brought freight and passengers to its dock to board steamers for San Francisco. Its natural attractions of sun and beach also kept a steady flow of tourists who often returned as residents to the area. However, soon after the sale of the railroad in 1877, the new owners abandoned the route and the steamers no longer stopped at Santa Monica. The town began to fade. The sale of lots dropped off, businesses closed and the town stagnated. The railroad rate war that began with the completion of the Santa Fe Railroad through line to Los Angeles in 1886 brought new immigrants to California and new interest in Santa Monica real estate. The town incorporated that year, and in 1887, a second auction was held to sell lots in East Santa Monica. Lots sold for as high as $1,350—a tidy increase over the first auction in 1875.

Among the renewed optimism of 1887 and increased western expansion, the Board of Managers of the National Home for Disabled Volunteer Soldiers was empowered by Congress to locate a site for a new home for Civil War veterans west of the Rockies. Sixty-one locations were offered for this purpose, including sites in Salt Lake City, San Bernardino, Inglewood, San Diego and the entire island of Catalina. The board, consisting of seven generals, two colonels and one captain, was royally entertained from San Diego to San Francisco. Each area wanted the $250,000 annual budget, along with the more than $60,000 in pensions, spent in its neighborhood, as well as the chance to provide the supplies needed for running the home. Senator Jones and R.S. Baker offered a three-hundred-acre site located on their Rancho San Vicente y Santa Monica, an additional five-acre site with a water source and $50,000 in cash. The site was number fifty-nine on the list. (Some land was also donated later by the Santa Monica Land & Water Company.)

The board members were undecided and during their meeting at the Palace Hotel in San Francisco seriously considered turning all the sites down and starting over. However, during their meeting they received a telegram from Senator Jones's lawyer increasing the cash offer by $50,000. The additional cash made the difference, and the board agreed to locate the Pacific Branch of the National Home for Disabled Volunteer

Fitch

Thomas Fitch was a well-known lawyer, politician and orator when he was picked by Senator Jones to launch the first auction for lots in his new town of Santa Monica. He defended such diverse clients as Brigham Young from polygamy charges and the Earp brothers and Doc Holliday from murder charges after the gunfight at the OK Corral. He wrote for numerous newspapers, was a contemporary and friend of Mark Twain and is credited with being one of the three great orators who kept California loyal to the Union during the Civil War. He held political office in four states—Arizona, California, Nevada and Utah—and practiced law in all of them. He was present when the Gold Spike was driven at Promontory Point, uniting the country by rail. As a staunch Republican, he campaigned for Lincoln across Nevada. He also helped draft the constitutions of both Nevada and Utah. He was elected as a congressman from Nevada in 1869 but was defeated in 1870 for a second term. He was editing the *Virginia Daily Union* in Virginia City, Nevada, when Senator Jones struck it rich, so they must have known each other there. In 1874, he had returned to San Francisco for a couple years before relocating again to Arizona.

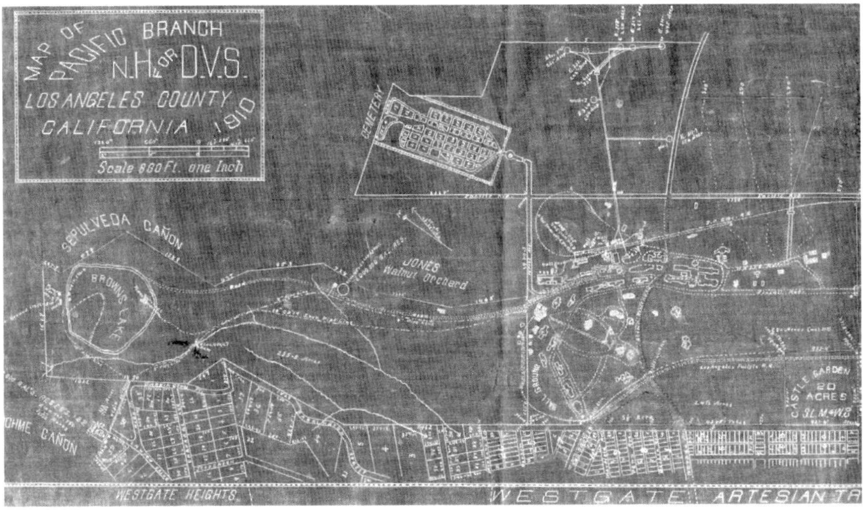

This Soldiers Home blueprint done in 1910 shows a thriving community of buildings, facilities such as a ballpark and the new subdivisions outside the West Gate.

Soldiers on the Rancho San Vicente y Santa Monica. With the arrival of Private George Davis, formerly of the Fourteenth New York Cavalry, who mustered in on May 2, 1888, Santa Monica secured a steady source of both residents and income.

The land was deeded "to locate, establish, construct and permanently maintain such branch of said National Home for Disabled Volunteer Soldiers." In order to limit the effects of strong drink on the soldiers, the rights to sell liquor were withheld on the land surrounding the home, a fact that complicated the transition from residential to commercial use in a later era.

Sawtelle

Families, veterans who did not need to live at the home and entrepreneurs catering to the needs of the home began to move into the area as soon as the new facility opened. They moved to Santa Monica, but soon a new development began to spring up around the southeastern boundary of the grounds. In 1896, Barrett Villa, named for the current head of the Soldiers Home, was laid out and the sale of lots began. When the post office rejected the name on the grounds that it was too close to another town's name, the investors asked banker and investor W.E. Sawtelle if he would agree to let them name the tract for him. He agreed, and Sawtelle it became. The

Pacific Land Corporation sold lots for eighty dollars to one hundred dollars each. Other investors included William T. Gillis and Robert Conran Gillis, whose wife was a relative of Sawtelle's. In order to get the trolley extended to Sawtelle, Senator Jones and R.S. Baker gave General Sherman 225 acres. To raise cash for the trolley, Sherman sold this tract to R.F. Jones and R.C. Gillis, who subdivided it as Castle Gardens. Members of the home were allowed to purchase and build in this area without losing their membership in the home.

Homes were built along cross streets named after Civil War battles—Vicksburg (now Stoner Avenue), Gettysburg (Colby Avenue), Chicamauga (Butler Avenue) and Mobile (Purdue Avenue). A business district grew up along Fourth Street (now Sawtelle Boulevard). Appomattox Drive remains to the present day as a last reminder of the "boys in blue." Soon there was a school, a post office and a bank. By 1901, there were 150 homes. The area was bustling.

The residents of the Soldiers Home were known to spend their pension funds on drink and other vices in Santa Monica. As much as Santa Monica tried to control the situation, the town developed a reputation for rowdy behavior, so much so that in 1900, an ordinance was passed to make Santa Monica a "no saloon" town. This had the effect of making Sawtelle the entertainment choice for the veterans. Gambling, prostitution and hard liquor sales all thrived in the little town outside the gates. The saying of the day about the residents was that "some sought heaven and some Sawtelle." Contemporary newspaper articles bemoaned the "horde of thugs, gamblers, prostitutes, and sellers of evil liquors…at the very gates of the Soldiers Home, for the pension money paid in large amounts to the old veterans."

Generally though, the pensioners were good citizens who tended the grounds of the home and minded their own business. Sailors docking at the Long Wharf often brought unusual plants and seeds to their friends at the home, giving the grounds a lush, tropical feeling.

Time eventually took care of the behavior problems, and Sawtelle morphed into a thriving Japanese/American enclave, with Japanese-oriented markets, restaurants and nurseries. The area continued as a center for Japanese American businesses until World War II, when the internment of the Japanese Americans disrupted the area, closing shops and restaurants. The residents returned after the war, and the area between Santa Monica and Olympic Boulevards retains its Japanese flavor with markets, nurseries, karaoke bars and shops.

Palms, Sunset, Ocean Park and South Santa Monica

Encouraged by the real estate boom, Palms and Sunset were laid out in 1887, Palms on the Rancho La Ballona and Sunset on the Rancho San Jose de Buenos Ayres. The communities were about five miles inland from Santa Monica and bordered the Southern Pacific line from Los Angeles to Santa Monica. The syndicate developing the Palms subdivision imported palm trees to use in the landscaping and to justify the community's name. Grand plans notwithstanding, Palms was mostly small ranches and farms until it was annexed to the city of Los Angeles in 1915.

The Los Angeles and Santa Monica Land and Water Company purchased the land for Sunset from J.W. Wolfskill. The investors included Senator Jones and R.S. Baker. Ten-acre lots were planned, as well as a large hotel and a town site. The Sunset subdivision was abandoned by its developers as the real estate boom of the 1880s waned. The hotel became a hay barn, and John W. Wolfskill eventually regained ownership of the land he had sold to them.

The arroyo (now the location of the Santa Monica Freeway) that divided the Santa Monica area in half formed a natural boundary for the area that became Ocean Park. Known originally as South Santa Monica, the area was mostly rural, although there were several attempts at subdividing during the boom of the early 1880s. One of the main attractions was the Kenilwoth Ostrich farm—a thriving petting zoo for the exotic birds. Edwin Vawter, son of Santa Monica pioneer W.D. Vawter, planted fifteen acres of land in carnations and roses on the heights at the top of Ocean Park and helped to develop a thriving flower market for local growers.

In the early 1890s, thanks to the efforts of Abbott Kinney and his partner, Francis G. Ryan, the beach frontage of South Santa Monica was developed into an attraction in its own right. A wharf was built for fishing and walking, a pavilion went up and cottages were developed for visitors to the beach. The area was advertised as the Coney Island of the Pacific. Lots cost about $100. A lottery was held as a promotion. The three winners won small four-room cottages. Tents were erected on unsold lots and rented to tourists each summer. With a donation of land from Kinney and Ryan and help from F.H. Rindge, the YMCA was persuaded to locate a facility in the area. In 1895, Kinney and Ryan named their new development Ocean Park. The Ocean Park Company donated land to build a bathhouse and an auditorium. By 1898, there were 150 cottages, and 40 more were added that year.

The area was poorly connected to the rest of Santa Monica and developed its own character independent of the rest of the city. There was also tension from the businessmen in North Santa Monica who were developing their own beach properties and did not like the competition. Concerned over these issues, Ocean Park briefly considered becoming independent in the early 1900s but remained part of Santa Monica.

Playa del Rey

Rancho Ballona had been partitioned into twenty-three separate parcels by 1868. Divided by two creeks, Ballona and Centinela, the land was mostly salt marsh and mud flats until the early twentieth century. In 1852, fifty inches of rain fell and put the whole area under water. The locals used it for duck hunting. A squatter called Will Tell had a sportsman's retreat for hunters at the mouth of the creek. Moye C. Wicks formed the Ballona Development Company in 1888 to develop a commercial port called Ballona Port. The Santa Fe Railroad began building a line into the area. It was the first attempt to dredge a harbor for Los Angeles. Three years later, the company went out of business with the end of the 1800s real estate boom and after finding it impossible to successfully dredge the lagoon for a harbor.

The area languished until General Sherman and E.P. Clark formed the Beach Land Company in 1902 with a group of fifteen investors that included R.C. Gillis, A. Fleming and F.H. Rindge. The group bought one thousand acres around the lagoon and laid out a community called Playa del Rey. The original intention was to install a network of canals and build a Venetian-style resort. Sherman and Clark built the "Short Line" to the new town in 1904, and tourists flocked to their new resort. A pavilion and a small hotel (in an Oriental, not Venetian, style) designed by architect Sumner Hunt and his partner, A.W. Eager, were built, and about a hundred lots were sold. The Balloon Route included Playa del Rey, bringing several thousand people into

~~HENRY P. BARBOUR,~~ President
M.H. SHERMAN, 1st Vice-President
ARTHUR H. FLEMING, 2d Vice-Pres.
P. M. GREEN, Treasurer
A. I. SMITH, Secretary

PLAYA DEL REY

DEL REY BEACH

THE BEACH LAND COMPANY

INCORPORATED

318 ~~219-220-221~~ CONSERVATIVE LIFE BUILDING

Corner Third and Hill Streets

Telephone Main 476

DIRECTORS
M. H. SHERMAN
E. P. CLARK
GEO. I. COCHRAN
ARTHUR H. FLEMING
JOHN D. POPE
R. C. GILLIS
~~HENRY P. BARBOUR~~

The Beach Land Company was formed in 1902 to develop Rancho Ballona into Playa del Rey. This letterhead lists directors including General Sherman, E.P. Clark, Arthur Fleming and R.C. Gillis. Henry P. Barbour was one of the original investors but was bought out by the others, hence his deletion.

Playa del Rey was newly built in this photo. A few visitors are arriving at the station in the foreground. The auditorium is built along with the pier. The lagoon is clearly visible in the center of the picture. *Courtesy of the University of Southern California on behalf of the USC Special Collections.*

the town each weekend. Luncheon at the hotel was part of the package. The Playa del Rey development also ran into competition with the North Santa Monica businessmen and their efforts at attracting tourists. Other attractions were added over the years, but gradually Abbott Kinney's Venice Beach (perhaps influenced by Sherman's original plan) became more popular. The entertainment attractions were eventually lost to storms and fire.

Playa del Rey has a Gillis Street with Gillis Beach at its foot. (There is also a Gillis Volleyball Tournament named for the beach.) It is the only piece of all the land subdivided by R.C. Gillis that bears his name. Today, the jets roar overhead and the houses have been demolished. The land is vacant and is a protected habitat for the El Segundo Blue butterfly. The streets will be torn out eventually, returning the land to its original state.

In 1916, the Army Corps of Engineers declared that the area was too expensive to develop as a port. In 1936, a reevaluation of the port idea was more favorable, but San Pedro received the financing instead of the Playa del Rey area. In the early 1950s, the City of Los Angeles and Congress came up with the funding to build Marina del Rey and a breakwater. The new marina was dedicated in 1965. It is the largest man-made small-craft harbor in the world. There are approximately 6,500 boats ported within the breakwater. The area also includes recreation areas as well as hotels and condos with beach views—close to the original plan laid out in 1902. The California Yacht Club, another Frank A. Garbutt project, was moved from Wilmington to Marina del Rey in 1967.

Santa Monica Land & Water Company (SML&WCo)

Baker died in 1894, but his interests in the Rancho San Vicente y Santa Monica had already been transferred to his wife, Arcadia. She and Senator Jones continued to develop the town. In 1897, they decided to form a corporation to hold their property in the Santa Monica area, apparently assuming that it would be easier to manage their holdings as a company as they grew older. The Articles of Incorporation were executed February 23, 1897. The corporation was formed

> *to acquire land by purchases or otherwise and sell the same; to acquire water and water rights by purchase or location or otherwise; to subdivide tracts of land into lots and blocks and sell the same; to erect building for any purpose; to erect and construct reservoirs and pipe lines for the purpose of saving and distributing water for domestic purposes, or for irrigation, and to furnish water to any town or city or the inhabitants thereof for household purposes or for any purposes.*

Arcadia Bandini de Stearns de Baker was issued 2,480 shares for her landholdings, and Senator Jones received 7,490 shares of stock for his portion of the land—roughly the same split as the original deal with Baker. The board of directors included Juan Bandini (Arcadia's brother), Roy Jones (Senator Jones's son), E.J. Gorham and Charles Forbes as the president of the board. (Forbes was Arcadia Bandini de Stearns de Baker's business manager.) The board agreed to provide water to the homes of Senator Jones and Arcadia Baker for free for their lifetimes. Robert Jones, the senator's brother, was the secretary, and his handwritten minutes document the first years of company activity.

Gorham resigned from the board in 1901, and R.C. Gillis was elected to take his place. Gillis would go on to purchase all of the stock of the Santa Monica Land & Water Company by 1904 and would continue to control it

The executives of the Santa Monica Land & Water Company in the 1920s. *Left to right:* C.L. Bundy, R.C. Gillis, H.E. Gorham, Louis Evans and Frank Lee. These men were responsible for many of the subdivisions in West Los Angeles. Gorham was Senator Jones's nephew. Bundy was one of five brothers who were all pioneers in Santa Monica. Louis Evans and Frank Lee were longtime members of the team. Lee started his own insurance agency in 1913.

until his death in 1947. Under his management, the company subdivided Brentwood, several areas of Santa Monica, Bel-Air and Pacific Palisades.

Interestingly enough, one of the first projects of the new company was the cultivation of lima beans. Ventura County was the center of this industry at the start of the twentieth century, but in 1902, Gillis planted an experimental plot near the Soldiers Home and discovered that the crop could produce about $45,000 per acre in net income. Lima beans were well suited to the cool, foggy climates of the Santa Monica area. By 1904, over ten thousand acres were planted and the income had topped $400,000. The beans were entered into an agricultural competition at the St. Louis World's Fair in 1904, winning the silver medal. Eventually the land was more valuable for homes, but lima beans provided a substantial portion of the company's income for a number of years.

Financing

Turning raw land into subdivisions is expensive The men who bought the land for this purpose needed to create infrastructure such as streets, curbs, sidewalks, sewers, water, electricity, gas hook-ups, lighting and landscaping and often other amenities like parks, sports facilities and business districts before they could attract lot buyers. Usually a syndicate of investors was put together to finance these improvements until sales of the land could begin. The investors would then be paid back through lot sales. The local banks often loaned the developers the money they needed or took mortgages on the land.

The quality of the infrastructure provided determined the income level of the new homeowners—the more lavish the improvements, the more money could be charged for the lots. The early developers did not build model homes or offer home plans to their purchasers. It was up to individual buyers to hire an architect or a builder to design and build their homes. Lot buyers often paid for their homes with mortgages carried by the developers, paying monthly amounts for their purchase.

The subdivisions and lots were sold with lavish advertising in the local papers and magazines of the day. In the early 1920s, Gillis and his investors formed a syndicate for advertising, running full-page ads in the Los Angeles papers that touted Santa Monica and Brentwood as wonderful places to invest in land, build houses and raise families.

Economic busts impacted the sale of land, punishing developers who suddenly had more land than buyers. Ghost suburbs—tracts laid out but never built because the lots could not be sold—were a fact of life in Santa Monica and Brentwood. The Pacific Palisades Association and the Pacific Land Company, developing the Huntington Palisades, were caught short by the Great Depression, and both developments foundered. The Pacific Palisades Association was taken over by its bond holders, the Huntington Palisades lot prices dropped dramatically and the development languished until after World War II.

Deed Restrictions/CC&Rs

Since the developers were not building homes, they attempted to control the look and feel of their subdivisions through deed restrictions. Lot owners were required to spend a minimum amount on their houses; they were required to observe strict setbacks for both their front and side yards. They were not allowed to sell any type of liquor; they could not raise or sell livestock for commercial purposes; they could not drill wells for oil or water for commercial purposes; and they could not operate stills.

Deed restrictions also limited who could purchase and live in the houses. The usual wording specified that homeowners could not sell their premises to any person of "Ethiopian, Chinese or Japanese descent." Sometimes the restrictions were worded that the owner could not sell to any person "not white or of the Caucasian Race." The wording reflects the mores of the day, and thankfully, the restrictions were voided by federal and state laws over the years, although they are still part of the deeds, startling homeowners who read their documents in detail.

Early on, there were only a few deed restrictions, but as time went on, they became more extensive with more architectural restrictions and rules. The Westgate deeds have four restrictions; Bel-Air Estates deeds have fourteen restrictions, including a provision for an architectural review by a committee designated by the developer. The Huntington Palisades deeds have several pages of restrictions.

Many of the developers also made provisions for covenants, conditions and restrictions (CC&Rs) that would be administered by homeowners' associations as the tracts were built out. The CC&Rs often control architectural designs, landscaping and the look and feel of the communities. Brentwood Park, the Huntington Palisades and Bel-Air all have strict CC&Rs.

The deed restrictions and CC&Rs have ensured that the original vision of the promoters and developers has been preserved and that the property values of the neighborhoods have continued to appreciate.

Other neighborhoods developed in Santa Monica during the early 1900s included Irwin Heights, Towner Terrace, Gillette's Regent Square, the Artesian Tract, Green Acres, Ocean Park Heights, East Ocean Park, Venice Park, Vineland, Serra Mesa and Clarkdale.

Westgate

The first real estate project that Gillis took on after buying the Santa Monica Land & Water Company was a residential subdivision bordering the west gate of the Soldiers Home. He called it Westgate and named the main boulevard of the tract San Vicente Boulevard for the original land grant. Street names reflected the officers of the SML&WCo—H.E. Gorham and C.L. Bundy—and eventually Gillis's daughter Dorothy.

Gillis worked with General Moses Sherman and his brother-in-law Eli Clark to construct a branch of the Los Angeles Pacific Railroad down the center of San Vicente Boulevard and connect it to the line serving Sawtelle and the Soldiers Home. Sherman was building a transportation system of electric cars from the center of Los Angeles to the burgeoning suburbs. In a letter to Gillis, he states his goals for the new road:

> *My Dear Bob,*
> *I have just talked with Mr. Clark about your matter* [San Vicente Boulevard] *down there and he is very much interested to help. I told him that you had a plan to make that the Finest Boulevard in Southern California (4 miles long). So that people would come from everywhere to see it. I have become very much interested in the whole matter and wish you might make oiled streets and make them as good as asphalt and people would come from everywhere to ride over them in their automobiles. Make the street wide, so as to have plenty of room for everybody…*
> *M.H.*

Over two hundred mules and horses graded the streets using Fresno Scrapers—a technology marvel of the day. The livestock ate tons of hay—bills show that 180,000 bales were purchased in a month for roughly $900. Larger lots were laid out near Beverly Drive (Sunset Boulevard); smaller lots were designated between Nevada Avenue (Wilshire Boulevard) and San Vicente Boulevard. The trolley trip to Los Angeles was supposed to take no more than thirty-five minutes. Lot prices started at $150, with five-acre lots going from $350 and up. The proximity of the Soldiers Home was touted as an advantage. The company planned to plant a thousand black Acacia trees along the streets. Early homeowners had room for their horses, cows, chickens and pets. They also had room for their newfangled automobiles.

The Westgate tract was joined by Westgate Acres and Westgate Heights, spreading homes across the area.

The Palisades

At about the same time that the Westgate development began, the SML&WCo formed the Alta Santa Monica Company and started development on the Palisades Tract north of Montana Avenue on the western edge of the Santa Monica mesa. At the time, the open land beyond Montana Avenue was used for pasture, for growing lima beans and as a place to ride ponies. It wasn't even part of the city of Santa Monica yet. Gillis visualized an upscale neighborhood for the businessmen of Los Angeles to build their beach homes—summer escapes from the heat and grit of the city.

Here the streets were named for the daughters and niece of the investors. Adelaide Drive along the rim of the canyon was named for Gillis's oldest daughter, then a fifteen-year-old schoolgirl. Marguerita Avenue was for Marguerita Drake, a niece of Arcadia Bandini de Stearns de Baker, whose

The call of the Mountains and The Sea

A marine view from a Palisades window

THE PALISADES
SANTA MONICA
THE ONE TINY SPOT IN
ALL THE WORLD

The place where you want to build your home. No matter what you have planned—a modest little bungalow or a mansion—there is no place where you can take advantage of all that Southern California offers like the Palisades of Santa Monica.

Pleasant surroundings with every modern improvement and convenience. Only forty minutes by auto out Wilshire boulevard from the center of Los Angeles.

An even climate the year round. Delightful in winter—cool in summer. That wonderful combination — the mountains and the sea — at your very door. A view that can never be taken from you.

Large well-located lots for as little as $900. Unequalled home sites up to $10,000. Terms arranged. SPECIAL INDUCEMENTS TO HOME BUILDERS.

SANTA MONICA LAND AND WATER CO.
1023 Investment Building
Los Angeles, Cal.
— or —
F. E. BUNDY, Agent
Second and Santa Monica Blvd
Santa Monica

This ad shows what the developers thought was important to prospective buyers: the bay, the beach and the views. The Indian seems to be there to emphasize the openness of the land. Note that F.E. Bundy was the selling agent.

father helped finance the development through his connection to the Los Angeles Trust and Savings bank. Georgina Avenue was named for Senator Jones's wife and daughter. Alta Avenue was named for the Alta Santa Monica Company.

The lots were one hundred feet by two hundred feet—big enough for tennis courts, garages for early cars and stables for horses. The early ads list many amenities like private alleys, water, gas, sewers, electricity and strict building restrictions. There were spectacular views of the ocean, the mountains and the canyon without the proximity of the railroad that ran along the bluffs at beach level. Access to the beach was facilitated at Inspiration Point by a staircase, which was eventually replaced by a small funicular that operated for several years. Sunset Park (now Palisades Park) was in easy walking distance. The SML&WCo donated the last strip of the park so that it could extend all the way to the end of the bluff. A series of oval parks was planned as part of the tract, but only one was built—now called Goose Egg Park.

The area became part of the city of Santa Monica in 1906. Lots were purchased by prominent Angelenos, including bankers, lawyers and judges, who built homes often using the best architects of the day.

Brentwood Park

The success of Westgate inspired another group of investors who purchased 350 acres of land from the SML&WCo and formed the Western Pacific Development Company. The price was $3,000 per acre. They named their development Brentwood Park after one of their bankers, William Lynton Brent. A park-like environment was designed by John McLaren, who designed Golden Gate Park in San Francisco. Eighty thousand trees and shrubs were integral to the plan. The tract improvements were estimated to cost half a million dollars. Plans called for thirty-two traffic circles and thirty-three larger traffic ovals with wide graveled and oiled streets. The advertisements touted large villa lots for $1,500. The trolley line down San Vicente Boulevard was an important selling point. Ads promised easy terms.

Deed restrictions and guidelines ensured a "natural and pastoral setting." There were no curbs, and the streets were laid out to follow the contours of the land. Other restrictions prohibited businesses of any kind, the distillation or sale of alcohol, billboards and oil wells. Almost all the lots had frontage of at least one hundred feet, and setbacks were supposed to be fifty feet. Houses had to be at least fifteen feet from the side lot lines. The Brentwood Park

Brentwood Park was planned with traffic circles and country lanes meandering over the landscape. There were supposed to be a number of trees and plants used in the landscaping, but many died or were never planted when the development hit hard times.

Improvement Association managed the landscaping and other improvements and continues to be active in the subdivision.

All of these careful plans were interrupted by the Panic of 1907. Unable to sell lots, the trees and shrubs were neglected and many died. The company was sold to Dr. Herman Janss (father of Harold Janss) who rescued it from oblivion and continued to sell lots. In 1916, it was annexed by the City of Los Angeles. As the city improved the streets, the original thirty-four traffic circles and ovals were reduced to eight. One more was lost when Sunset Boulevard was realigned. At the same time, the city straightened many of the streets and added curbs, destroying some of the country park atmosphere.

Gradually, the land around the original developments in Westgate was subdivided into neighborhoods—Brentwood Circle, Brentwood Country Estates, Brentwood Glen, Brentwood Heights, Brentwood Sunset, Brentwood Terrace, Kenter Canyon, Mountaingate, Brentwood Hills and Brentwood Highlands, to name a few.

In the 1920s, A. Bell, who was one of the first graduates of Occidental College in Eagle Rock, set aside land north of Beverly Boulevard (Sunset) as a new men's campus for the school. The project was to be funded by the sales of lots in a development called Tigertail Estates. The student body protested the idea of a men's campus separated from the main campus, and eventually the Depression derailed the plan. However, Tigertail Road takes its name from the school's mascot—Oswald the Tiger.

The area was annexed to the city of Los Angeles in 1916. Over time, it became more known as Brentwood than Westgate until today the original name only exists as Westgate Avenue.

Brentwood/North Santa Monica

The SML&WCo continued to subdivide its land along San Vicente Boulevard during the 1920s and '30s. San Vicente Park, Brentwood Canyon Estates, Brentwood Place and Brentwood Terrace are all bounded on at least one side by San Vicente Boulevard. The real estate hyperbole of the day promised ocean views, contoured lots versus rectangular plots, mature trees and developer-funded improvements. Prices continued to climb with the years, and lots close to San Vicente were selling at $2,500 by the mid-1920s. However, Gillette's Regent Square, developed by King Gillette of razor fame, was laid out in 1911 but had only sold five lots prior to 1920. Brentwood Park did not take off until the promoters' advertising push in the 1920s.

The Canyon Vista Park tract was laid out in the early '20s along the Santa Monica Canyon rim. La Mesa Drive is a mere six blocks long between Nineteenth and Twenty-sixth Streets, but it was designed to be one of the most exclusive areas of Santa Monica. Dorothy Gillis Loomis is responsible for the landscaping and the planting of the dramatic Moreton Bay Fig trees that form a leafy corridor on the street. She and her family lived on the street for a number of years. The thirty-seven houses are on large lots and were designed by the leading architects of the day. Many of the homes have sweeping canyon and mountain views and overlook the Riviera golf course. A favorite pastime of the children during the '30s was to throw firecrackers onto the greens from the canyon rim.

Santa Monica Canyon

At various times, SML&WCo purchased sections of the Rancho Boca de Santa Monica to add to its holdings. The mesa below the canyon bluffs was part of one of those purchases. For a long time, the land was used for lima beans and duck hunting. In the early 1920s, business leaders in Santa Monica offered the area to General Arthur MacArthur as a site for summer army maneuvers. Fortunately, he didn't take them up on that one.

Evans and Reeves

Hugh Evans was born in Stamford, England, to parents who surrounded their home with plants and were dedicated gardeners. Taking his cue from his parents, Evans chose to study at an agricultural school and then immigrated to San Luis Rey in San Diego County—a colony of English expats. He struggled with a small lemon ranch and a nursery but gave them both up to become a successful real estate and insurance businessman. His most famous development was the Wilshire-Fairfax tract, now known as the Miracle Mile. He built a large Craftsman-style home in 1925 on three acres in the Brentwood Place tract in Santa Monica. He landscaped the home with a bountiful garden and soon was sharing plants with his friends.

The garden attracted visitors from all over the world, and he experimented with many new varietals and plants brought to his door by his friends. There were over 150 varieties of hibiscus and many types of fuchsias and cymbidiums. He was a member of the board of governors for the Botanical Garden in Mandeville Canyon. The bougainvillea plants he propagated were so popular that he started a nursery as a sideline.

His real estate business failed during the early years of the Depression, and he turned to his gardening hobby for income. In 1931, he began wholesaling plants from his private garden to local nurseries. In 1936, he and his sons teamed with Jack Reeves, son of another nurseryman, to start Evans and Reeves Nursery in Brentwood. For the next twenty years, the nursery was ground zero for the landscapers and homeowners of West Los Angeles, providing new and unusual plants and influencing the gardens and streetscape of the city. Clients included many of the Hollywood elite. Evans was a major impetus for using the colorful coral trees as the centerpiece of San Vicente Boulevard as a replacement for the trolley tracks. Evans died in 1960, leaving as his epitaph the many colorful plants he brought to California.

His son Morgan "Bill" Evans carried on his father's tradition, becoming the landscape architect for Disneyland. His imaginative design and use of plants transformed eighty acres of Orange County into five enchanted lands defined by their exotic and colorful plantings. He remained a consultant for Disney for many years, working on Disneyworld and EPCOT Center in Orlando, as well as the Tokyo and Paris parks.

In 1926, the land was deeded to Dorothy Gillis Loomis and Robert Lindsay Gillis. A tract map was filed shortly thereafter for a development to the north of Seventh Street. One of the streets was to be named Lindsay Road, since he was the only Gillis sibling without a street named for him in West Los Angeles. However, the post office required a change, and the name became Kingman Avenue. San Lorenzo Street and Channel Road are the other main streets. The tract also included the Marquez family cemetery, which was preserved by the SML&WCo. Dorothy Loomis asked John Byers to build an adobe wall as a boundary around the small cemetery plot and purchased a statue of St. Lorenzo for a niche he designed into the wall. Eventually the cemetery was returned to the Marquez family and is recognized by the Los Angeles Cultural Commission as Historical Cultural Monument 685.

Below Adelaide Drive, lots were sold in the early 1900s along Mabery, Entrada and Rustic Roads. The streets wind around the trees and the flood channel. The area appealed to an eclectic group of writers, actors and artists and was home to a number of well-known people. Christopher Isherwood is

In 1924, Santa Monica Canyon was mostly open land near present-day Seventh Street at the right of the picture. Adelaide Drive runs along the rim of the canyon in the lower right-hand corner. San Vicente Boulevard is in the upper right-hand corner. The Canyon Mesa tract would be developed in the open area in 1926. In the center of the photo, the Marquez cemetery is visible. Riviera Country Club had not yet been built.

one of the best known—he had several homes in the canyon, including one on Adelaide Drive above the canyon. He describes the canyon residents as "tacky and cheerful and defiantly bohemian, tirelessly inquisitive about each other's doings, and boundlessly tolerant" in his book *A Single Man*.

A small commercial district eventually replaced the tents, campsites and bathhouses of the early beach-going Angelenos who came each summer to camp in the mouth of the canyon. It included a pharmacy called Doc Laws for many years. The story goes that he dispensed prescriptions out the front door and bootleg liquor out the back. He was known to supply booze for Will Rogers and other local residents during Prohibition.

Pedro "Pete" Badilla

Pedro M. Badilla was the son of Pedro P. Badilla, who came to California in 1812 and was granted a rancho near Santa Barbara. Pedro, who was known locally as "Pete," lived in Santa Monica Canyon and was considered a character by the residents. Dorothy Gillis Loomis remembers thinking he was pirate when she was a child. She recollected that he lived down in the canyon in an "overgrown cottage with a parrot." Apparently she was half right: he actually worked for the Secret Service (part of the Customs Department) and was tasked with chasing down opium smugglers in Malibu. Later on, he was active in enforcing the Prohibition laws against bootlegging.

Rustic Canyon

In 1887, Abbot Kinney donated part of his Santa Monica Heights property (on the mesa that became Huntington Palisades) to create an experimental forestry station. He was the first chairman of the State Board of Forestry. H. Rowland Lee of the University of California was put in charge of the station. In 1889, Senator Jones and Arcadia Baker gave the Forestry Service another eighteen acres in Rustic Canyon to enlarge the agricultural station. The station studied and experimented with plants that might thrive in the area. Eucalyptus trees were a special part of the project. The Santa Monica Heights land was heavily planted with these trees, many of which survive today. The State Board of Forestry was disbanded in 1893, and the U.S. Department of Agriculture took over the station. The area was planned as an arboretum and public garden, but eventually it was abandoned and the land subdivided. Recently, the Rustic Canyon section of the original station has been designated a California Historical Landmark and is now a small park.

The Uplifters was a social club started by a group of Los Angeles Athletic Club members. Their goal was to "uplift the arts." The group purchased more than sixteen acres of land in Rustic Canyon as a place to hold their meetings and activities. Eventually the area was subdivided, and the log cabin homes that are still evident in the canyon are the group's contribution to the landscape.

Sam Carson

There were many squatters on the ranchos that covered West Los Angeles. One of the better-known ones was a man called Sam Carson who claimed he was the nephew/son of the famous scout Kit Carson. Sam Carson lived in Rustic Canyon in a makeshift camp for a number of years along with his dog and horses. He made a living cutting

Sam Carson lived in a tarpaper shack in Rustic Canyon with his horses and dogs. He claimed to be Kit Carson's son and that the rifle he has on his lap was his famous father's long rifle. *Courtesy of the Santa Monica Public Library Image Archives.*

firewood in the canyon and selling it to the more settled residents. He also raised bees and sold the honey. He often sold wood to R.C. Gillis, who used to joke that he was paying for wood cut on his own land. He was something of a legend in his own time. Visitors brought him food, and Dr. Phillip Lindsay, Gillis's brother-in-law, took care of his health. After one bout of illness, as payment he gave Dr. Lindsay a long rifle that he claimed had belonged to his famous uncle/father. The rifle is signed by H. Carlile on the barrel. In 1902, a group of good Samaritans bringing Carson food found him dead in his bed from a spider bite. (Other accounts say he died from eating putrefied meat from a dead cow.) Friend and neighbor Pascual Marquez buried him in the Marquez family cemetery.

Author's note: Research has not turned up documentation that Sam Carson was indeed the nephew or son of Kit Carson. Contemporary newspaper articles seem to accept that he could be who he said he was, but they also seem somewhat skeptical. He claimed to be both the son or the nephew of the scout over the years, but there is no record of Carson having a nephew/son named Sam that matches the dates or that he was ever in Galveston, where Sam claimed to have been born. H. Carlile was a noted gunsmith working in Shippensburg, Pennsylvania, from about 1818 to his death in 1847. The Carson family lived in Booneslick, Missouri, during Kit Carson's childhood, having followed the Boone family there. Long rifles were prized possessions, so it is possible that this rifle was purchased in Pennsylvania and traveled with the family to Missouri and beyond.

Sullivan Canyon

R.C. Gillis retained Sullivan Canyon for his own personal use after selling much of the contiguous land to Alphonzo Bell. He built a stable at the mouth of the canyon and a cabin farther back into the canyon. The stable housed the horses for the family and also Adelaide Gillis McCormick's prized Kentucky American Saddlebred horses. The cabin was used both as a retreat for Gillis and often as a meeting place for his executives. During the 1920s and '30s, Dorothy Gillis Loomis and her Mexican and Japanese helpers grew gladiolas at the mouth of the canyon and chives up near the cabin.

When World War II broke out, Dorothy moved her family—her husband, one daughter still in school, her daughters-in-law (whose husbands were in service in the South Pacific) and her mother-in-law—into her father's cabin and the house vacated by the Japanese farmer who had been interned. She grew vegetables and had a milk cow, chickens and a turkey. Her small farm provided food over and above wartime rationing for her family and also for her parents living in Hancock Park.

Gillis deeded the canyon to Adelaide Gillis McCormick in the late 1930s, and after the war, she decided to relocate to San Diego County. The land was sold to Cliff May, who relocated to Los Angeles from San Diego. Bell had shown him the property and urged him to buy it. He subdivided the canyon as Riviera Ranch, designing and building many of the homes for the new owners. He built several homes for his own family in the canyon as well, using them as living laboratories for his architectural theories. Sullivan Canyon retains its rural vibe, and many of the families there still have horses.

Pacific Palisades

By the early 1920s, the Rancho San Vicente y Santa Monica was almost totally subdivided. Developers began to look at the mesa beyond Santa Monica Canyon—the Rancho Boca de Santa Monica—for more development. The Chautauqua movement began in New York in 1874 as an adult education program designed to bring culture, arts, music and intellectual stimulation to communities across the country. Independent Chautauqua sites were created around the country, usually outside small towns. The movement provided a traveling troupe of players, musicians, lecturers, speakers and other forms of entertainment. In Los Angeles, there were successful encampments in Huntington Beach and Long Beach in the early part of the 1900s. By 1921, these sites were being crowded out by their rapidly developing communities. To solve this problem, a search was instituted by the Methodist bishop to find a more permanent site. The Reverend Charles Scott was picked to lead the search. He was offered several different sites but eventually settled on the land on the Rancho Boca de Santa Monica mesa, north of Santa Monica.

In 1922, over fifty thousand people rose early and took a special train to Santa Monica to celebrate Easter with a sunrise service. The advertising for the event billed Santa Monica as the "Chautauqua of the West." The Pacific Palisades development was not yet named or viewed as separate from the city of Santa Monica.

Scott formed a group of "Founders" to assist him with financing and developing his new permanent Chautauqua site on the Rancho Boca site. The first meeting was held in the Broadway Department Store in June 1921. He formed the Pacific Palisades Association and appointed 25 distinguished Angelenos as trustees. The Founders were developers and investors in the West Los Angeles area—R.C. Gillis, Henry Chandler, General Moses Sherman, Paul Shoup, Arthur Letts, May Rindge, H.E. Huntington, E.P. Clark, Albert Wallace, Walter Armacost, Charles Clarke Chapman and Andrew M. Chaffey, to name a few. The association raised the money to purchase 1,100 acres of the mesa, and in January 1922, the 275 Founders

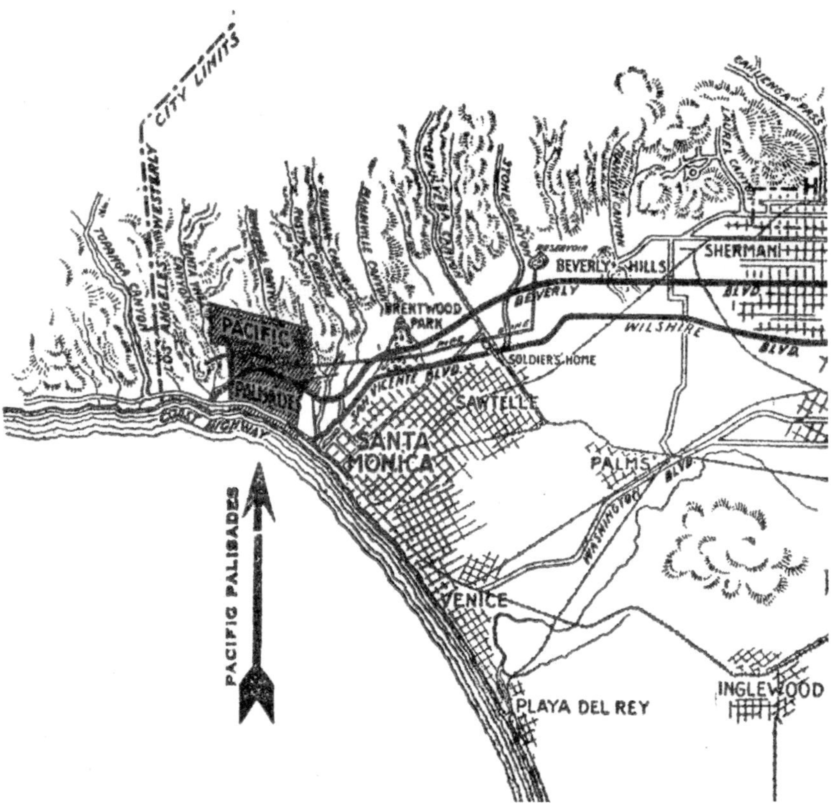

This map was used on the 1923 Pacific Palisades Association brochure for its Series B, Sinking Fund General Mortgage 7 Percent Gold Bonds. The flyer states that the association has already expended $5 million for eleven miles of concrete sidewalks and gutters, two and a half miles of streets surfaced with rock and oil, electric light and telephone service and a high-pressure fourteen-inch Los Angeles Aqueduct water main. Note the presence of Beverly Boulevard through the new neighborhood. That did not happen until 1926.

and trustees were allocated lots in the new development. Improvements were estimated at $4 million. The Methodist Church took the lead in founding the community, but the community was open to everyone and was nonsectarian. The name was a nod to the bluffs that met the sea below the mesa. It was also a way to tag along with the Santa Monica Palisades tract, which was older and much better known.

The Chautauqua facilities were created in cool tree-lined Temescal Canyon. There were rustic *casitas* as accommodations for the attendees, a large communal dining hall and a library. In addition to the Chautauqua facilities, the association intended to subdivide the mesa into homesites and offer them to founders and others on ninety-nine-year leases. The revenue from the lots was intended to fund the Chautauqua activities. As the developers, the association made the improvements to the tract, laying out cement sidewalks and curbs and hooking up to the Los Angeles water, electricity and gas. Advertising mentions that lots could be purchased for as little as 20 percent down. The prices started at $2,000. The tract maps show smaller, more affordable lots north of Beverly Boulevard (Sunset Boulevard) and larger lots to the south of the boulevard. The smaller lot area became known as the alphabet streets. These streets were named for Methodist ministers in alphabetical order. By the end of 1922, the association had leased $100,000 worth of property, and by 1926, some 250 families were living in the area.

Huntington Palisades

Abbot Kinney purchased the land on the edge of the mesa that became Pacific Palisades from the Marquez family early in his Los Angeles career and planned a tract called Santa Monica Heights. He laid out the roads and planted a number of eucalyptus trees along the contours of the land. He intended to make it the "Nob Hill of Santa Monica," even planning a railroad up the canyon for transportation. However, the subdivision was never built. Collis P. Huntington, of Southern Pacific fame, was the next owner. He intended to build a large mansion overlooking the Long Wharf he had built at Potrero Canyon below the bluffs, but the idea died with the wharf.

Henry E. Huntington, nephew of Collis P. Huntington, owned the Red Car system of interurban trolleys. At his uncle's death, he married his widow, who inherited an interest in the land on the bluff. The land became available for sale in 1925, and the Catholic Church was seriously considering purchasing it as a site for a private girls' college. The Pacific Palisades Association decided to purchase the property in 1926 to prevent

The Huntington Palisades was developed with sixty-foot-wide streets, underground utilities, decorative lighting and naturally contoured streets. It was intended to be a high-value neighborhood. In this photo taken in the 1940s, there are some homes but also many empty lots. The house in the foreground was designed by Pierpoint Davis.

the school from competing with its fledgling development. The price was $1,625,000 for 230 acres of land—about $7,500 an acre. The plans for the new tract named for the Huntingtons were ambitious. They included sixty-foot contoured streets, ornamental lighting, curbing, undergrounded utilities and strict deed restrictions. The costs would eventually top $1 million. There were even dreams of a bridge crossing the canyon and linking the Santa Monica bluffs and the Pacific Palisades mesa. That plan was dropped during the Depression.

The Huntington street names were selected by Wilkie Woodard, the engineer who laid out the tract. Most of them were taken from Mexican mines where he had he worked, except for Alma Real Drive, which was named for his favorite Mexican singer.

Arthur Fleming was instrumental in one of the largest lot sales in the Huntington Palisades when he persuaded his McCormick relatives to purchase twelve lots on the rim of the mesa as a summer home for Cyrus

McCormick's mentally ill daughter. Mary Virginia McCormick lived most of her life under close custodial care in a number of specially built homes. The estate in the Huntington Palisades included a house, a music facility, a guesthouse, a large garage and a staff of nurses and musicians. Due to its proximity to the bluff, the McCormick family spent a great deal of time and money trying to prevent landslides below the property. The property was broken up at Mary McCormick's death but is often still referred to as the McCormick Estate.

The Pacific Palisades and the Huntington Palisades thrived until the stock market crash in 1929. The subsequent Great Depression deflated real estate values and discouraged people from purchasing real estate so far from the center of Los Angeles. The Pacific Palisades Association dissolved, and lots were sold instead of leased. The community became a residential suburb with less emphasis on the Chautauqua movement. R.C. Gillis ultimately took over the Huntington property and completed the improvements. The SML&WCo was the selling agent for the tract and built several spec houses in the area. The real estate picture did not improve until after World War II, at which point the area began to grow again, ultimately reaching its potential (and Abbott Kinney's original vision) in the 1960s.

Bel-Air Estates

The Rancho San Jose Buenos Ayres—or Wolfskill ranch, as it was known by the turn of the century (after the brief experiment with subdividing the Sunset town area)—was used primarily for agriculture until developer and oil man Jake Danzinger purchased land in the hills and built a large home in 1914 overlooking its fields. Danzinger spent about $1 million on the mansion and the grounds surrounding it, building a tennis court, golf course, pool, stables and a trout hatchery. He called the estate La Quinta. The Danzingers divorced in 1923, and the property was purchased by Alphonzo Bell after a fire threatened his family at his home in Santa Fe Springs. The house was renamed Capo di Monte (top of the hill). From there, the views included the ocean and the city of Los Angeles.

By 1922, Bell owned about twenty-two thousand acres of land purchased from Danzinger, the Santa Monica Mountain Park Company and the Santa Monica Land & Water Company. He formed the Los Angeles Mountain Park Company to manage his holdings. The land included some of the Rancho Boca de Santa Monica and the Rancho San Vicente y Santa Monica and the hills of the Rancho San Jose Buenos Ayres.

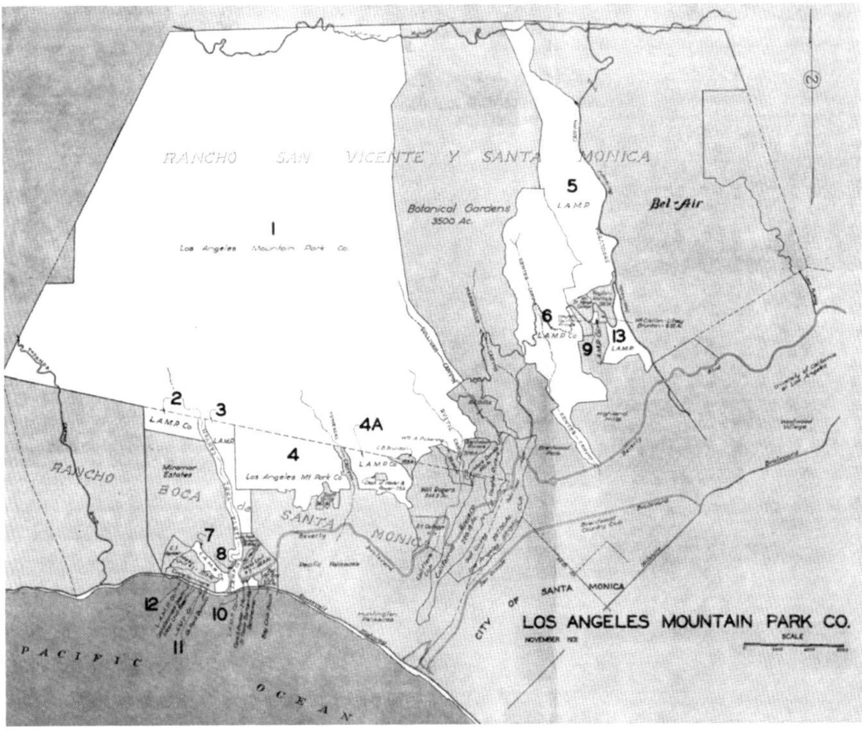

This map shows the properties of the Los Angeles Mountain Park Company owned by Alphonzo Bell. The developments that are already underway are the gray sections.

After a trip through Italy, Alphonzo Bell and his wife were enthralled with Italian culture and architecture. He saw the West Los Angeles area as similar to the Italian countryside he had seen. (In fact, Southern California is very similar in climate to southern Italy and France.) His wife translated the Spanish "Buenos Ayres," meaning "beautiful airs," to the French "Bel-Air," a neat play on both the rancho and Bell names. Bell began to develop his landholdings into an upscale elite neighborhood with the highest standards for wealthy Angelenos. The advertising touted "a community of gentleman's estates." The street names picked by Bell's wife were a tribute to Italian towns, and the lots were large (minimum of one acre). Homes needed to be worth at least $20,000. The subdivision was one of the first with underground utilities and other amenities. Rock walls that terraced roads and hills were built with stone quarried from the property. Bridle trails and tunnels were built under the roads to keep horses and cars on separate tracks. Two wrought-iron gates, part of the original development,

LOS ANGELES MOUNTAIN PARK CO.

Southern California's Most Beautiful Residential Properties

DIRECTORS
ALPHONZO E. BELL
FRANK L. MELINE
A. B. RUDDOCK
EUGENE OVERTON
HAL A. LLOYD
CLAUDE A. WAYNE
GARNET C. RAINEY

Office of the Salesmanager
JAMES V. WESTERVELT

1142 PACIFIC MUTUAL BUILDING
523 WEST SIXTH STREET
Telephone MUtual 2215
LOS ANGELES, CALIFORNIA

PARK OFFICE
10601 CHALON ROAD
ADMINISTRATION BLDG.
BEL-AIR, LOS ANGELES
OXFORD 1175

Letterhead for the Los Angeles Mountain Park Company shows the directors and the address of the park office on Chalon Road.

still provide access to the community and its winding roads. Lush planting was added to provide privacy to the residents who eventually included a number of prominent movie industry executives and stars, as well as political and business luminaries. Bell's home included a garage for his sophisticated collection of autos, a stable, a pool and a hillside landscaped to replicate the Tower of Babylon.

Bell's strict Scots Presbyterianism colored his rules for his subdivisions and clubs. Originally, no real estate could be sold on Sundays. The clubs were dry until after the repeal of Prohibition, and Bell did his best to prevent the movie industry from infiltrating his development. No Jews or non-Caucasians were allowed. The restrictions limited sales and were gradually dropped as the Depression took hold.

Bell also developed the Bel-Air Country Club, its golf course and the Bel-Air Bay Club on the beach in Pacific Palisades.

The Riviera

One of Bell's other projects was the sale of more than 600 acres in the hills and Santa Monica Canyon to the Los Angeles Athletic Club for the purposes of creating a golf club. The plan was to subdivide the land—then planted with a grove of lemon trees—around the site to finance the club. The Frank Meline Company was selected as the selling agent for the 386 homesites laid out on 227 acres. Lots were one hundred feet wide and three hundred feet deep. There were a number of deed restrictions designed to ensure a pleasant neighborhood and protect the residents' investments. The street names commemorate Italian towns—Amalfi, Capri and Napoli—and reflect Bell's influence on the subdivision.

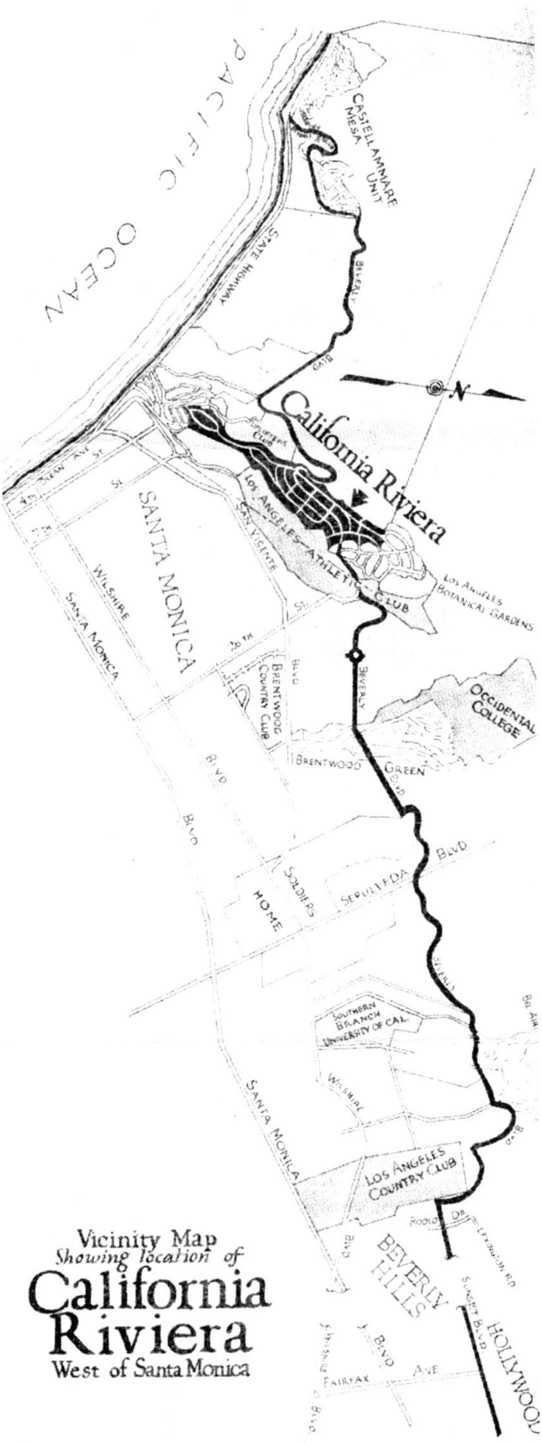

The original offering for the Riviera development syndicate by the Frank Meline Company promised a 7 percent dividend for those who bought in. The map shows the proposed Botanical Gardens and the proposed Occidental College site. The area marked Los Angeles Athletic Club shows the proposed Riviera Country Club golf course and polo fields.

Mandeville Canyon

Originally this area was called Casa Viejo Canyon after the creek that runs through it. The Mandeville name appears about 1900, apparently taken from a squatter who once lived in the canyon. The neighborhood started out as the California Botanic Garden. In 1926, the Garden Foundation, Inc. acquired 3,200 acres of land from the Santa Monica Mountain Park Company, intending to dedicate 800 acres as a botanic garden. According to the brochure, the goal was "that the Garden may remain forever free from political interference or need of seeking charity, the raw land comprising the endowment fund are being improved and converted into cash by release to persons desiring country estates overlooking one of the greatest gardens of its kinds in the world."

The officers and directors of the Garden Foundation included Alphonzo Bell and R.C. Gillis, as well as a distinguished group of directors including Harry Chandler, Douglas Fairbanks, Mary Pickford and William Randolph Hearst.

The garden was planted with tropical trees and flowers, and several large pools were constructed, but lot sales lagged and then dried up as

The logo for the California Botanic Garden illustrates the high hopes of its developers.

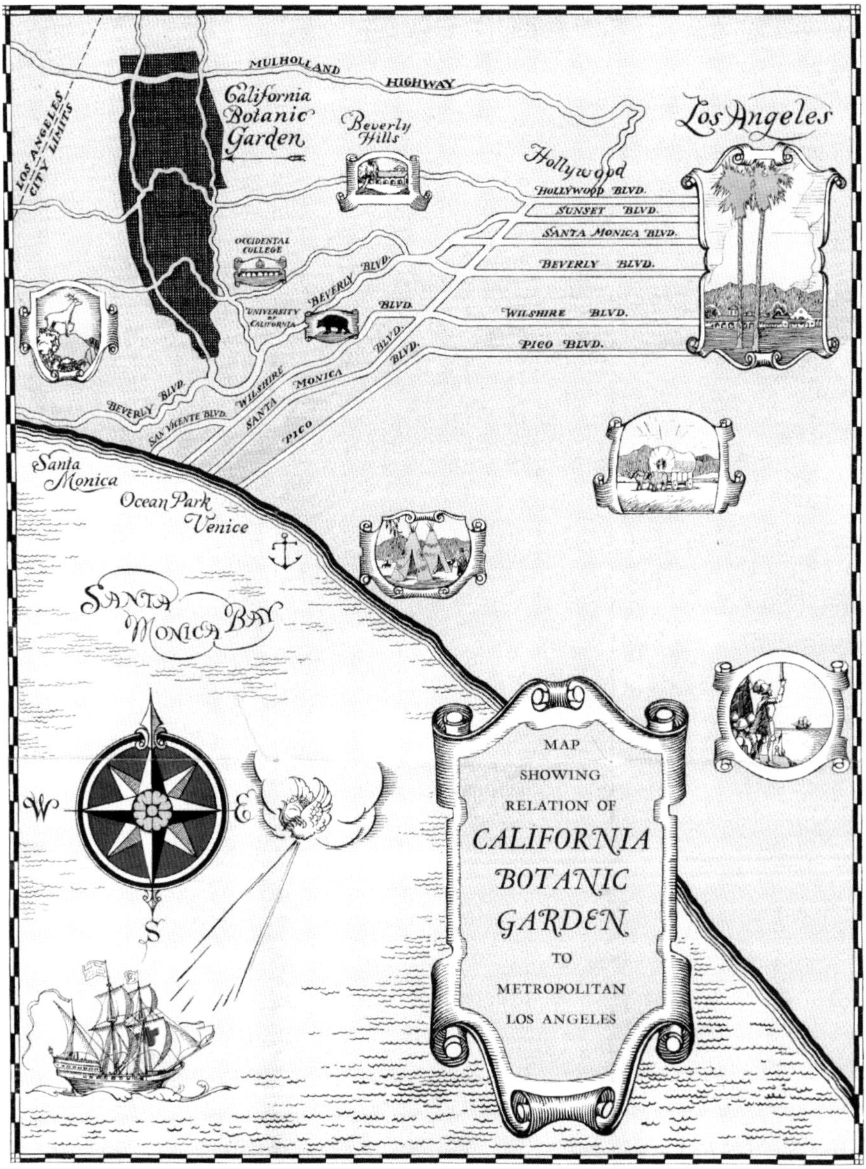

The Mandeville Canyon brochure touts lofty goals and a long list of directors. The area was planned as a tropical garden with lush plantings as well as homes built into the canyon. The lot sales were intended to fund the garden, but the Depression derailed the plans.

the Depression hit. The Los Angeles Athletic Club purchased the area at the mouth of the canyon as an extension to the Riviera Country Club and developed its equestrian facility (now Paul Revere Charter Middle School). There were eventually three polo fields, stables and grandstands on the property. Soon the polo crowd purchased lots in Mandeville to stable their polo ponies. Horse owners would ride across the canyons behind Sullivan and Rustic to play with Will Rogers on his polo field. The Garden Land Company incorporated in 1932 to hold the property when the Garden Foundation lost the land to its bondholders. The Garden Land Company sold the first large-scale development in the canyon (three hundred lots) in the 1950s.

Castellammare

Bell's Italian theme continued with Frank Meline's (Bell's sales agent) Castellammare development at the end of Beverly (Sunset) Boulevard and the Pacific Ocean. The name means Castle at the Sea and reflects the steep hillside character of the neighborhood. The streets are again named for Italian towns—Revello, Posetano and Bellino. Steep stairs connect the streets as well as the winding roads. Residents have access to the beach by pedestrian bridges constructed across the Coast Highway as part of the original development. Breathtaking ocean views were a selling point. It was a requirement that homes be designed in the Italian Renaissance style. A commercial center was constructed near the highway to serve the residents. The Villa Leone was one of the first homes built in the area and became a well-known landmark for drivers on the Pacific Coast Highway. It was built by Leon Kauffman, and its ram motifs reflect his background in the wool industry. The area is prone to landslides, and more than one home has gone down the cliffs over the years, along with parts of streets and sidewalks.

Malibu

The Tapia family was prominent in Los Angeles and owned several ranchos in different areas. It is likely that they did not spend much of their time on their Rancho Malibu. There is a tale that Tiburcio Tapia buried several chests of coins on the rancho just before he died suddenly. He never told anyone where he hid them, and they have never been found. The remote rancho was a haven for cattle and horse thieves and smugglers. It often appears in the court records of the day in conjunction with chases and arrests. In 1857, the land was purchased by Mathew Keller, a prominent Angeleno who, among other things, is credited with planting one of the first vineyards in Southern California. The price was reported to be between ten dollars and twenty-two dollars an acre. He built a large ranch house on the Malibu property and made some improvements. At his death in 1881, the rancho went to his son, Henry W. Keller, a prominent resident of Senator Jones's new city of Santa Monica.

In 1891, Keller sold the rancho to Frederick H. Rindge, who also lived in Santa Monica. Rindge was looking for "a farm near the ocean, and under the lee of the mountain, with a trout brook, wild trees, a lake, good soil, and excellent climate." His wife told him he wanted too much, but he found his ideal "farm" in the Rancho Topanga Malibu Sequit. Rindge added other parcels of land to his Malibu holdings and eventually owned twenty-four miles of seacoast. His land extended three miles inland and covered over seventeen thousand acres. Rindge located his home in Malibu Canyon and was often in residence until the house was destroyed by fire in 1903. After the fire, Rindge moved to Los Angeles but was still active in Santa Monica and his beloved Rancho Malibu.

There were no roads through the Rancho Malibu—everything had to come in by boat or horse-drawn wagon at low tide. The Southern Pacific

In order to prevent the Southern Pacific from pushing its tracks through his land, Frederick Rindge created his own railroad. The trestle in the picture was a triumph of engineering. The Rindges prevented the railroad from crossing their ranch, but eventually the Pacific Coast Highway was constructed across their land. *Courtesy of the Santa Monica Public Library Image Archives/Title Insurance and Trust Collection.*

wanted to build a railroad link between Santa Barbara and its terminus at the Long Wharf through the rancho. Rindge refused to give it a right of way. Instead he started his own railway—the Hueneme, Malibu and Port Los Angeles Railroad. (California law did not allow a right of way for a duplicate line paralleling an existing line.) After Rindge's untimely death in 1905, his wife, May Rindge, continued her husband's plans.

Fifteen miles of track were laid for ranch use. Hides, beef and grains were shipped to the Rindge pier—now Malibu pier. It operated for about twenty years. May Rindge has the distinction of being one of the few women to ever serve as head of a railroad. The narrow-gauge short line prevented the Southern Pacific from obtaining a right of way and made sure that the railroad tracks turn inland at Oxnard north of Malibu instead of running along the coast through Malibu.

May Rindge prevented the Southern Pacific from building a rail line but fought a long and ultimately losing battle against the public road that the state intended to put through her ranch. The struggle took over twenty years through numerous courts, including the U.S. Supreme Court. The road was finally opened in 1929. The struggle and May Rindge's fierce fight to keep the Malibu private earned her the title "Queen of the Malibu" and a lot of bad press. It also preserved the Malibu as a distinctive residential suburb with unlimited beach and mountain views.

One of Rindge's other ventures was the Malibu Potteries started in 1926. Using local clay and the plentiful water available on the ranch, the potteries produced many tiles and other decorative items during their six years of operation. The colorful distinctive tiles were often used in the Spanish Colonial–style Los Angeles homes built during the '20s and '30s. Large panels of the tiles were used in Los Angeles City Hall. Samuel Rodia, the builder of the Watts Towers, worked in the potteries and often took home chips and scraps of tile to add to his project. A fire and then the Depression doomed the potteries, and they closed permanently in 1932.

Rindge's daughter Rhoda May married Merritt Huntley Adamson. He started Adohr Stock Farms—Rhoda spelled backward—one of the largest dairies in the country. The Adamson House, built in 1930, was their home until Rhoda May's death in 1962. The house contains many outstanding examples of Malibu tiles and is now open to the public, thanks to a fourteen-year effort to place it in the National Register of Historic Places and save it from being turned into a parking lot.

The first land development subdivision on Rancho Malibu was the Malibu Colony. As a promotion for the lot sales, the developers offered some of the land to movie stars on ten-year leases. The stars liked the idea, and the colony quickly became a hideaway for the rich and famous. Small cottages were built and used by the likes of Ronald Coleman, Delores del Rio, Jack Warner, Gloria Swanson, Gary Cooper and many more. Eventually the leased land was sold to the actors, and the Malibu Movie Colony became a permanent home to celebrities, rock stars and movie stars.

Venice Beach

Abbot Kinney continued developing his property south of Santa Monica after the sale of his property north of Santa Monica. Kinney's first partner, Frank Ryan, died unexpectedly in 1898, and Kinney went through several groups of partners with mixed results. In 1904, the current group agreed to dissolve their partnership and divide the development with the toss of a coin. Kinney's then partners—Alexander Fraser, Henry Gage and George Merritt Jones—assumed Kinney would take the Ocean Park portion of their holdings if he won the toss. Kinney did win the toss but surprised them by taking the salt marshes on the southern end of the property. That land would become Venice of America—a premier beach resort and destination.

He began developing this marshy area as a resort patterned after Venice, Italy. The drainage ditches used to drain the marshes became several miles of canals. His new resort included a hot salt-water plunge, an auditorium, a ship-themed restaurant and a dance hall. He constructed a business street patterned after a Venetian arcade. There were also cottages and tents for the tourists who wanted to stay on the wide sandy beach. The town would often have 50,000 to 150,000 tourists on weekends. The area continued to be called Ocean Beach until 1911, when the name was officially changed to Venice Beach. Over the next few years, Kinney added an aquarium, the Virginia Reel Whip, the Racing Derby and other attractions to his beach community. Kinney died in 1920. The pier burned a month later but was rebuilt with better and more extensive attractions—two roller coasters, a Glass House (a maze of mirrors) and other rides. The Coal Mine attraction featured burros pulling carts of tourists through a tunnel. A third roller coaster was added in 1925, along with a Dragon Slide, where visitors climbed to the top of the tower and slid down on bamboo mats. The Flying Circus whirled riders around a sixty-five-foot tower, giving them an experience close to flying. Tourists were deposited on the beach from the trolley car system in droves. Venice was the Disneyland of its era.

The area continued unincorporated until 1925, when it was annexed to Los Angeles.

Gold Coast

Santa Monica's beach frontage is known as the Gold Coast, but it was more of an unwanted stepchild in the early days of the area. The SML&WCo owned most of the beachfront from the municipal pier to Santa Monica Canyon. Lots had been subdivided above the beach on the hills near the mouth of Santa Monica Canyon in 1899, but the strip of land between the bluffs and the high tide line was considered too narrow to develop. R.C. Gillis and the SML&WCo offered the strip to the City of Santa Monica for $25 a front foot. The offer was turned down. At that point, the SML&WCo decided to install groins or jetties along the beach to build up the sand and widen the beach. After the beach was widened, it was again offered to the city for $75 a front foot and again turned down. At that point, the company subdivided the area into lots and sold the land to private owners for summer homes. Movie actors

This ad for Palisades Beach touts the area that became better known as the Gold Coast, with many movie industry moguls and stars purchasing property.

The names and locations of some of the original famous owners of the Gold Coast as well as the locations of many of the beach clubs and piers are shown in this photo.

and moguls quickly saw the value of the area and snapped up the lots. One lot sold for $1,700 per square foot, far exceeding what the city would have paid.

Many celebrities and famous people have lived in the houses of the Gold Coast. President John F. Kennedy visited his sister and brother-in-law—Peter Lawford—during his presidency, putting the enclave in the national headlines. By far, its most notorious resident was Marion Davies, the mistress of William Randolph Hearst. Hearst built a large mansion for Davies with several guesthouses, and they entertained the rich and famous on her beach at Santa Monica for a number of years. Other luminaries who lived on the Gold Coast included J. Paul Getty, Douglas Fairbanks, Irving Thalberg and Norma Talmadge.

Westwood

Arthur Letts, the founder of Bullocks and Broadway Department Stores, purchased 3,300 acres of the Wolfskill ranch in 1919. (Roughly the area that was originally subdivided as Sunset in 1887.) He paid the Wolfskill heirs $500,000 in a certified check and another $1,500,000 when the title was transferred to him. His intention was to change the barley and bean fields into a mixed development with retail stores, apartments, homes and a university. As a trustee of the State Normal School, he pushed to move it from its outgrown small campus to his new community. He christened the area Westwood and Holmby Hills after his ancestral home in England. His son-in-law Harold Janss took over the project and launched the subdivision in 1922. Janss was the vice-president of Janss Investment Company, and he successfully completed his father-in-law's vision for one thousand residential and commercial lots. The streets were given English names in honor of Letts's background. The community was planned with homes for the wealthy and middle class. There were no liquor restrictions and fewer deed restrictions than Bel-Air Estates. Hollywood stars were welcome, and religion was not considered. Singer Rudy Vallee was an early owner. The only real requirements were money and taste.

In the mid-1920s, the University of California at Los Angeles had outgrown its site on Vermont Avenue. The Janss family offered to build a college town if the university would move to the open fields of the Westside. A. Bell donated $250,000 to the board of regents as part of the push to move the school to West Los Angeles. The Beverly site, as it was called for

Westwood Village started as a shopping area for the University of California at Los Angeles and quickly became a major retail and entertainment area for West Los Angeles.

its proximity to Beverly Hills, was selected in 1927 over competitive sites in Palos Verde and Pasadena. The land was purchased from the Janss Investment Company for $1 million, roughly one-third of its value. The day after the selection was made public, thousands of people visited the site. The company sold over $1 million worth of lots in the next four days.

The Westwood Village shopping district was built in 1929 to coincide with the opening of the new university. Arthur Letts Jr. built his home in Holmby Hills in 1927. The mansion was purchased by Playboy Enterprises in 1971 and became the Playboy Mansion.

Crestwood Hills

One of the more unusual neighborhoods that developed north of Sunset Boulevard in Brentwood is Crestwood Hills. After World War II, there were many young couples looking for places to live and establish their families. Several friends, musicians for the studios, came up with the idea of pooling their finances and buying a piece of land. They would then subdivide it among themselves and build homes. When they researched their idea, they discovered that they could be considered a community if they had four hundred families signed up for their idea. As a community, they would be eligible for utilities, schools and shopping facilities. The idea became a reality when the original four families grew to five hundred. The group bought eight hundred acres of land two miles north of Sunset for $400,000. In 1948, each family paid $2,000 for membership in the newly incorporated Mutual Housing Association. A contest was held to select the name, with Crestwood Hills winning the honor.

From its beginnings, the community had plans beyond just houses. They set aside eleven acres for a park, created a cooperative nursery—still in operation today—and opened a credit union. They also created a truck garden to grow vegetables and planned a shopping center. The group wanted modern designs for their homes that took advantage of the terrain and the vistas it provided. Architects Whitney Smith and A. Quincy Jones were asked to create several sets of plans. Members could choose a plan suited to the orientations of their lots and their needs. The architects created twenty plans, and eventually over a hundred homes were built using their designs.

The community was not in agreement with the then accepted ethnic deed restrictions imposed by the owner of the land they purchased, but it accepted some in order to buy the land. These restrictions were not heavily enforced as the community developed. They did impose design restrictions on members to ensure that homes were painted in colors that enhanced the development and were designed in a modernist style.

The community held regular holiday celebrations and potlucks for the residents in its park. Eventually the association gave the park to the City of Los Angeles in return for its development and maintenance. The park became Crestwood Hills Park, and the city built a clubhouse to go with the pool the community had built.

There is also an open-air theater named for longtime Crestwood Hills resident Fritz Feld. Feld starred in over four hundred movies, as well as many TV shows and radio programs. He took an active part in creating the plays and concerts held at the Fritz Feld Community Playhouse. Feld and his wife, Virginia Christine, the original Mrs. Olson of the Folgers Coffee commercials, often entertained the musicians and performers who came to the playhouse to perform.

Chapter 3
BUILDERS

California Style

The early buildings in West Los Angeles were simple adobe dwellings made with local materials and without much thought to style. That changed when the promoters began to subdivide the land into house lots. The built environment—the houses and buildings where people live and work—is the most important point of contact for most Westsiders. There are a potpourri of architectural styles, colors and sizes—Craftsman, Bungalow, Beaux Arts, Old English Manor, Mission Revival, Spanish Colonial, Monterey, ranch, modern, post modern and deconstructionist. Some of the architects who built this environment were self-trained; others had degrees from distinguished schools that included Harvard, Massachusetts Institute of Technology and L'Ecole des Beaux-Arts in Paris. The buildings are the sum of their design skills and their understanding of how architecture responds to its environment. Their buildings reflect the influence of the climate and geography of California and its many layers of settlement. Some of the best architectural minds and trendsetters of their eras designed homes at the behest of the far-thinking developers and residents who created the communities of West Los Angeles.

Myron Hunt/ Elmer Grey

The Palisades development in Santa Monica was intended to be an upscale retreat for Los Angeles businessmen who lived in the city. The idea was to subdivide the area above the beach into lots on which they could build summer homes as a place to escape from the hot, dusty city. One of the first houses built there was for the tract developer R.C. Gillis. In 1905, he engaged Myron Hunt and Elmer Grey, who had recently formed a partnership in Pasadena. Both men were from Chicago. Hunt was an early member of the Prairie School and shared an office for a short time with Frank Lloyd Wright. He moved to the Los Angeles area in 1903 in the hopes of restoring his wife's health. Grey was an award-winning architect by age eighteen and had made a name for himself with his summer home built at Fox Point in Wisconsin. He was well on his way to becoming a prominent architect when his health failed, and he moved to California. The two men became friends and partners and in 1904 formed the firm of Hunt and Grey.

The house on Adelaide Drive was one of their first commissions together. According to the 1905 *Architectural Record*, "Both Mr. Hunt and Mr. Grey stand for the attempt to naturalize in this country the best traditions of European architecture." They are often credited with evolving a distinctive California style synthesizing traditions that influenced many of their contemporaries.

In another early magazine article, the Adelaide Drive house is described as a "Town House with Opportunities for Outdoor Living." The article goes on to describe the house as having a courtyard arrangement that was "similar to the patio of an old Spanish House." All of the rooms of the

An early picture of the beach house designed for R.C. Gillis by Myron Hunt and Elmer Grey on Adelaide Drive. Note that the rooms all open onto the outside courtyard.

house opened onto the interior courtyard, reflecting its use as a summer retreat. (Eventually this open corridor was closed in.) The article concludes that Hunt and Grey are designing homes that are "closer to the Craftsman idea than any other." Grey's design vision, as he described it in 1907, was that "the best California bungalow schemes involve a garden or large outdoor living space incorporated as an integral part of the plan."

The architects also applied their distinctive philosophy of simplicity and naturalness to several other styles—Beaux Arts, Mission Revival and English Tudor—modifying them for the California climate and lifestyle.

Hunt and Grey developed a number of homes in Pasadena and Los Angeles, including Henry E. Huntington's home in San Marino. That house reflects their evolving California style with its red tile roof and sage green window trim. The team also designed dormitories for the new campus of Occidental College in Eagle Rock and several of the buildings for Troop Polytechnic Institute (California Institute of Technology). They designed the Ambassador Hotel as well. Eventually, Grey's health problems broke up the partnership, but on his recovery, he went on to design the Bel-Air Bay Club for A. Bell and houses in the Canyon Vista tract. He also designed the Beverly Hills Hotel.

Hunt also had a distinguished career with his next partner, Harold C. Chambers. He was the primary architect for Occidental College until the 1940s. He also designed the original Huntington Hotel, the Rose Bowl and the Pasadena Library.

These two architects and their design philosophies had a substantial influence on their fellow architects and the look and feel of the homes and buildings in West Los Angeles.

Pierpoint Davis

Francis Pierpoint Davis was born in Baltimore, the son of an architect. He and his brother Walter also became architects and moved to Southern California in 1905. Another brother, Henry, became a landscaper. Pierpoint apprenticed with his father, while Walter studied at Massachusetts Institute of Technology (MIT) and toured Europe on an MIT traveling scholarship. He joined his brother in California in 1912, and they founded the firm of Davis and Davis.

Pierpoint Davis was a founding member of the Garden City Company of California. The members of the group were committed to "the designing and building of beautiful homes and gardens, the consistent architectural development of real estate subdivision, and the layout of such subdivisions

Pierpoint Davis designed this gracious home as a sample of what types of homes would be the norm in the Huntington Palisades. The center court was built around the eucalyptus tree planted in Abbott Kinney's earlier development.

and town sites." In 1916, the group published *Ideal Homes in Garden Communities* with a set of designs that took advantage of California's climate and advocated year-round garden living. The homes pictured in the book, many designed by Davis and his brother, are simple with an abundance of windows overlooking garden areas. They often have interior patios. The influences of rural Italy and Spain, as well as Italian and French Renaissance architecture, are clear in their designs. Their designs anticipate the ranch houses of the 1950s. Davis designed one of the first homes built in the Huntington Palisades for R.C. Gillis as an example of the homes that could be built there. The firm also designed many courtyard apartments.

Sumner Hunt

Sumner P. Hunt was raised in Brooklyn, New York, and came to California in 1888. One of Hunt's first residential projects was a home for Roy Jones on Ocean Avenue in 1894. The house was built in the American Colonial Revival style—simpler than the Queen Anne style that had been popular prior to that time. (The house is now the Heritage Square Museum.) It is the first example of Hunt using this style. He also designed the North Beach Bathhouse located at the bottom of the Ninety-Nine Steps in 1894. Hunt went on to design many distinguished homes in Los Angeles.

Robert David Farquhar

Robert Farquhar was born in Brooklyn, New York, and educated at Harvard and MIT. He also attended the Ecole des Beaux-Arts in Paris from 1896 to 1901. He practiced architecture in New York and then moved to Los Angeles in 1905. He was of the architectural commission that designed the San Francisco Panama Pacific Exposition in 1915 and was responsible for its Festival Hall. Farquhar married Marion Jones, the daughter of Senator Jones, in 1903. He designed a Spanish Colonial home for H.E. Gorham on Adelaide Drive and a home for his own family on Georgina Avenue. The Henry Weyse/Charles Morris house on Ocean Avenue is a melding of Colonial Revival and Craftsman styles. It was built in 1910. Farquhar also designed the Beaux Arts California Club in downtown Los Angeles and was part of the team that designed the Pentagon in Washington, D.C.

John Byers/Edla Muir

John Byers started his career as an electrical engineer, graduating from the University of Michigan and then going on to do graduate work at Harvard. He worked for two years with the United States Commission at the Paris Exposition and then switched gears to teach languages in Montevideo, Uruguay, and San Rafael, California. In 1916, he took a job teaching French and Spanish at Santa Monica High School. His introduction to California architecture seems to have come about through his language skills. His wife's cousin was building a house on Rockingham Avenue and needed a translator for the Mexican crew who were camped near Santa Monica Canyon and Seventh Avenue. Since he was known for doodling buildings while his students were taking tests, it seemed natural for Byers to help with the design as well as the communication issues. The workers showed him how they made roofing tiles by shaping the clay over their thighs and how to use adobe. He was fascinated with the shadow pattern made possible by the uneven shapes of the tiles and the possibilities of adobe as a building material.

Soon he was designing adobe and tile homes for his family. In 1919, he set up a tile kiln on Colorado Avenue to make roof and floor tile. His first professional commission was for Santa Monica High School principal W.F. Barnum, and by 1922, he had quit his job as a teacher to work full time as an architect. Byers's interest in adobe, tile and Spanish architecture coincided with the rise of the Spanish Colonial style popularized by the opening of the Panama Canal and the subsequent expositions in San Diego and San Francisco in 1915. Byers's attention to detail and his use of adobe or brick painted to look like adobe quickly became popular.

His workshop made decorative tile, wrought iron and woodwork. At this time, he called his company "John Byers Organization for the Design and Building of Latin Houses." He also incorporated tile made by the Malibu Potteries on the Rindge ranch into his homes. When the large timbers he needed were scarce after World War I, he scavenged lumber from the demolition of the Long Wharf. His client list quickly included the famous—he designed houses for Shirley Temple and Joel McCrea and a ranch house for J. Paul Getty. One of his most typical houses is the L.L. Bradbury house on Ocean Way. He built his own Monterey-style home on La Mesa Drive and built several other homes along that street. The Miles Playhouse in Lincoln Park (now Christine E. Reed Park) in Santa Monica is also his work. In his later career, he partnered with Edla Muir to build English Tudor and other styles of homes. Despite their varying influences, all of his designs have similar attributes—French doors to patios and galleries, double fireplaces and a feel for their relationship to the California climate.

The Ranch House

Cliff May

Clifford Magee May was born in San Diego. He was related to several of the original Californio families (Bandini, Carrillo and Estudillo) and grew up around the haciendas of Old Town San Diego and the Santa Margarita (now Camp Pendleton in San Diego County). He was not trained as an architect but started designing Monterey-style furniture and progressed to designing adobe homes in San Diego. His first buildings owe much to the adobes and rancho homes in which he spent his childhood—U-shaped layouts, overhangs that protect doors and walls and open *corredors* to connect rooms. In the early 1940s, May purchased Sullivan Canyon from Adelaide Gillis McCormick and began to perfect his "ranch" style. He is generally credited with popularizing the ranch house that became so prevalent in California and the rest of the country in the 1950s.

Needless to say, there were many architects contemporary to May who also designed with an emphasis on the relationship of their buildings to the outside and for the California climate. However, May's slab foundation building technique made the ranch house a household name. He engineered a way to pour a concrete slab as a foundation instead of a basement or pier and beam construction. His goal was to design living areas, kitchens and bedrooms that let residents walk directly outside onto the ground without descending steps. He also wanted a warmer floor for his homes. He accomplished both goals with his design for a sealed slab foundation. It was also cheaper to build, and when it was approved by the Federal Housing Administration and the Veterans' Administration, it rapidly spread all over the country as an inexpensive building method for the homes needed after World War II. May worked closely with *Sunset Magazine*, and its many articles on his homes contributed to his popularity.

His homes feature high ceilings, often open-beamed, with skylights; large expanses of glass walls that open up to the outside seamlessly without steps onto patios; cross-ventilation; and a high degree of livability. He is credited with promoting the sliding glass door and many other innovations taken for granted today in home building. His houses combine the best of the early California homes and intersect with the modernist style of the twentieth century. May built his own home in Sullivan Canyon, and many other homes in West Los Angeles are built to his plans and there are many imitators. May was a licensed building designer until late in his life, when he was licensed by the State of California as an architect. He was proud of the designation but always deprecated his achievements. As he put it, "I was just busy building homes."

Case Study Houses

Arts & Architecture Magazine sponsored the Case Study Houses from 1945 through 1966, eventually sponsoring the design of thirty-six prototype houses. The idea was to develop plans for affordable housing without sacrificing good design in the post–World War II world. John Entenza, the magazine's editor, was an advocate for modernism, and he attracted a group of like-minded architects to design the homes—Schindler, Stahl, Neutra, Eames, Koenig and Saarinen all participated. Many of the designs were actually built in Los Angeles—eight in West Los Angeles—and the plans and pictures of the homes were published in the magazine.

Richard Neutra

Richard Neutra was born in Austria in 1892 and was educated at the Vienna University of Technology. He worked in Germany at the beginning of his career and then immigrated to the United States in 1923. He worked briefly with Frank Lloyd Wright and then came to Los Angeles in 1925 at the invitation of his friend Rudolph Schindler. Neutra designed Case Study House #20 for the Bailey family on a bluff above Chautauqua Boulevard. It is a small home, but it impresses with its wide expanses of glass opening onto uninterrupted views of the outdoors. Neutra's stripped-down designs were a reaction to the Baroque excesses of his native Austria. In this house, walls and doors are fitted exactly without the coverings of decorative moldings and frames—a challenge for its builders, who had to make each corner and door frame perfect. Neutra was known to work closely with his clients to make sure that his homes were livable and comfortable.

Time magazine used Neutra on its cover in 1949, comparing him to Frank Lloyd Wright. He designed over three hundred houses and coined the term "biorealism" to describe "the inherent and inseparable relationship between man and nature." In addition to his Case Study House #20, he designed many other houses for West Los Angeles owners.

Charles and Ray Eames

Charles Ormonde Eames was born in 1907 in St. Louis, Missouri. He studied at the Washington University of St. Louis on an architecture scholarship but left the university reportedly because his admiration for Frank Lloyd Wright clashed with his professors' views. Other sources say he was working full time for an architectural firm and that impacted his studies. He was friends with Eero Saarinen, son of Eliel Saarinen. The older Saarinen was a director at Cranbrook Academy of Art and invited Eames to study there. It was there that he met his second wife, Ray Kaiser. She was from California, and they relocated to Southern California in the 1940s.

Eames built Case Study House #8 on a lot close to Neutra's Bailey house on the bluff in Pacific Palisades. The house is notable because it was built by hand of pre-fabricated parts meant for industrial construction. The house became both a home and work space. In addition to its unusual building materials, the house is known for its economic living spaces, outdoor enclosed spaces and views of the Pacific. Its steel frame is considered a precursor to the high-tech buildings common today. The use of steel and glass ties the house to the International style of Mies Van de Rohe—open planning, precise simple detailing, neatness and a light quality. Eames's goal for this house was livability—it is partially buried to take advantage of the slope, sited to take advantage of the natural ventilation from the sea breeze and shaded by a deep roof overhang and grove of eucalyptus trees probably planted by Abbott Kinney.

Ray Eames was an artist in her own right and was very involved in the iconic furniture designs that Eames made for Howard Miller and their other artistic endeavors. The Eameses were also involved in the design of Case Study House #9 (also in Pacific Palisades) with their friend Saarinen. This house was owned by John Entenza, the originator of the Case Study Houses project. Charles Eames was never licensed as an architect but continued working on architectural projects until the 1960s.

The Others

Frank Gehry

Frank Owen Gehry was born in Canada in 1929 and moved to Los Angeles in 1947. He is well known for his ability to deconstruct architectural forms into their separate elements even as they enclose the space for homes, museums, concert halls and commercial buildings. His childhood was spent using scraps of building materials from his grandfather's hardware store to create houses and science fiction cities. That experience gave him intimate knowledge of the everyday building materials that he would use in his projects. He tried many jobs before he settled on architecture, receiving his degree from the University of Southern California. He briefly studied at the Harvard Graduate School of Design but found it too confining for his ideas of socially responsible architecture. He is known as a post-modernist, deconstructionist or a post-structuralist for his unorthodox use of materials and space.

His home in Santa Monica stopped traffic when its remodel was completed in 1978 and launched his career as an avant-garde deconstructionist designer. He removed the walls, pushed out skylights and revealed the structure of the house. His use of chain link, plywood and metal as part of a remodel for a rather ordinary Cape Cod house startled Santa Monica and jarred the neighborhood of small suburban California houses that surrounded it. It was very controversial but definitely prefigured his public buildings, like the Disney Concert Hall and the Guggenheim Museum Bilbao in Bilbao, Spain.

He was selected to design Santa Monica Place in 1980 (remodeled several times and changed from his original design) and has done numerous other projects in West Los Angeles.

There were many architects and contractors who built homes and buildings in West Los Angeles over the years. Greene and Greene, Frederick Roehrig, H.X. Goetz, the Milwaukee Building Company, the Wilson Brothers, Paul Williams, Wallace Neff and Frank Lloyd Wright all contributed to the visual texture of the neighborhoods by building distinctive homes for the residents of the growing community.

Chapter 4
GETTING AROUND

Sixty-eight thousand acres is a lot of territory, and in order for the area to thrive, there had to be a transportation system for the residents. The original residents walked, rode horses or drove carriages or ox-pulled carretas. The trip from Los Angeles—some twenty-five miles away—was hot and dusty and took all day. The rancheros, although they were required to have houses on their properties by the terms of their grants, kept houses in town and only came to their ranches for short visits. Dorothy Gillis Loomis and her sister Adelaide Gillis McCormick remembered driving their pony carts loaded with dogs and supplies from their house at Twenty-eighth Street and Severance downtown to their beach house on Adelaide Drive at the beginning of each summer. However, by about 1906, their father was driven about in his chauffeured Locomobile instead of a horse-drawn runabout. By the early 1900s, Sherman and Clark were rapidly expanding their Los Angeles and Pacific Railway into West Los Angeles.

Transportation was about to change, and Los Angeles was about to become a streetcar and automobile city.

Trolleys

The Red Cars

The first attempt at mass transit in Santa Monica was a horsecar line running along Ocean Avenue. It ran from present-day Colorado Boulevard to Third Street over to Nevada and from there to the Soldiers Home. It was started by

The Pasadena and Pacific Railway Company was the first streetcar company that General Sherman and his brother-in-law E.P. Clark purchased in Los Angeles. The company was given the first franchise to bring electric streetcars to Santa Monica in 1896. Shortly after this event, the name was changed to the Los Angeles Pacific Railroad. Note the change from Los Angeles to Sherman, another of General Sherman's developments—now West Hollywood.

Williamson Vawter and his sons. General Sherman's Pasadena and Pacific Railway Company acquired the franchise to run an electric trolley line into Santa Monica in 1896. It opened for business in April of that year and was soon renamed the Los Angeles Pacific Railway. Santa Monica declared a half-day holiday, and the whole town partied at the terminal. It quickly became so popular that the Southern Pacific and Santa Fe Railroads saw their passenger business drop to almost nothing.

Playa del Rey opened for lot sales in 1902, and Sherman began work on connecting a trolley line into his system to carry passengers there immediately. It started running in 1904. Westgate became part of the trolley system when the line opened from Sawtelle to San Vicente Boulevard in 1906. Eventually the Los Angeles Pacific and its successor, the Pacific Electric, crisscrossed the entire West Los Angeles area with an efficient transit system that facilitated the sale of lots and made it possible for the new residents to move around the city quickly and easily.

Beach Access

Sunset Trail/ California Incline/Ninety-Nine Steps

Transiting from the top of the bluffs at Santa Monica to the beach has always required a steep climb of one sort or another. Over the years, various solutions have been used to make the beach more accessible to the bluff. At first, a dirt path was cut from the bluffs to the beach below for horses and pedestrians. It was known as the "Sunset Trail" and located at the foot of

Montana Avenue. Arthur Loomis used to relate a story about how he often took a Model T Ford up the trail to the top of the bluff as a shortcut from the beach. One of the times he did it, he was met by two Santa Monica motorcycle policemen at the top who arrested him and threw him into the local jail. Judge J.J. Carrillo (Leo Carrillo's father) convened his police court very early the next morning (before the police started their day). He asked Loomis if he had done it and, after he admitted it, dismissed the charges with a stern warning, saying, "Arturo, you have been a very bad boy. Don't do it again, time served." The trail eventually became a staircase that still exists today.

The California Incline was originally called Linda Vista Drive. Located at the intersection of Ocean and California Avenues, the incline extends 1,400 feet from the top of the bluffs to the Coast Highway. It is shared by pedestrians, bicycles and automobiles and is often used as a backdrop for movies. It is still one of the main access roads from the bluffs to the Pacific Coast Highway.

In addition to the Sunset Trail, there was a wooden staircase from Palisades Park to the beach called the Ninety-Nine Steps. Built in 1875 at the foot of Arizona Avenue, the steps allowed pedestrians to cross above the Southern Pacific tracks and eventually over the Pacific Coast Highway. The wooden steps were replaced with concrete ones in 1935 and continue to provide access to the beach from Palisades Park.

The Arcadia Hotel originally had a gravity railroad to bring guests from the train station on the bluff down to the hotel. The Thompson Switchback Gravity Railroad was an early type of roller coaster. Ten people could ride it at a time, and it cost five cents for a round trip. Eventually, the coaster was replaced by wooden steps. There was another gravity railroad located at Inspiration Point at the end of Palisades Park. This funicular was replaced by several sets of steps down the canyon wall from Adelaide Drive. Another set of steps from Vance Street in Pacific Palisades connects walkers to Rustic Canyon. Tunnels under the Coast Highway at the mouth of Santa Monica Canyon allow pedestrians safe access to the beach under the Pacific Coast Highway. There are also steps that connect Castellammare to the beach (as well as each level of the development) built as part of the original tract in 1927.

Avenues, Boulevards and Freeways

Ocean Avenue

Ocean Avenue runs from Adelaide Drive at its northern end to Pico Boulevard at the southern end of Santa Monica. Ocean Avenue was bridged to Ocean Park across the arroyo that separated the two parts of the town in 1886. Lined with stately palms, it parallels Palisades Park and offers spectacular views of Santa Monica Bay and glorious sunsets. When the grid for Santa Monica was laid out, Ocean Avenue was the spine of the new city. All of the major east–west roads in Santa Monica terminate here.

Originally it was lined with eucalyptus trees planted by J.W. Scott, developer of the Arcadia Hotel, and cypresses. Dorothy Gillis Loomis remembered her shock when the original trees were all cut down and replaced with the palms that now line the avenue. Senator Jones built Miramar, his large mansion, on Ocean Avenue; Baker built a Victorian home for his wife, Arcadia; and Roy Jones, Abbot Kinney, H.W. Keller and Frederick Rindge all built homes on Ocean Avenue. Over the years, the stately single-family homes gave way to the current tall buildings with condos at the north end and hotels, restaurants, offices and shopping centers at the south end. Senator Jones's home is gone, but its name survives on a luxury hotel. (The hotel is called Miramar, like the house.) The street has been widened several times and is always busy. It remains the spine of Santa Monica and one of its main thoroughfares. Route 66 officially ends at the intersection of Lincoln and Olympic Boulevards, but there is a plaque placed at Ocean Avenue and Santa Monica Boulevard commemorating its terminus in Santa Monica.

Wilshire Boulevard

Wilshire Boulevard started as an animal trail following the path of least resistance at the base of the Hollywood Hills and the Santa Monica Mountains in search of food and water. The tar pits along the way captured the unwary, leaving a fossilized record of the saber-toothed tigers, antelope, deer and bears that traveled the trail. The native peoples used the trail as they roamed the area. The Spanish padres and explorers called it the "Camino Viejo"—the old road. It became known as the "Brea (tar) Road" in the early 1800s. The tar seeping up from the ground was useful for waterproofing roofs and calking boats. Oxcarts hauled it laboriously down the widening trail across the Rancho San Vicente y Santa Monica to the Shoo Fly Pier

Nevada Avenue and Bundy Drive were trails in 1906, but Nevada Avenue would eventually become the mighty Wilshire Boulevard of today. C.L. Bundy and L.D. Loomis were working on the Westgate subdivision in this photo taken in about 1906 and seemed to have stopped in the shade of the eucalyptus trees for a meeting.

located on the land that would become Santa Monica. From there, it was shipped to San Francisco and other points along the coast.

As Los Angeles grew, the trail widened again to become the horse-and-buggy route to the Pacific beaches. R.S. Baker and Senator Jones saw the advantages of the road connecting their ranch and Los Angeles. In their plan for Santa Monica, it was renamed Nevada Avenue for the senator's adopted state. In 1895, with the profits from his first development efforts in Orange County, Gaylord Wilshire bought thirty-five acres of land in the Los Angeles area, including the Brea Road. He donated the right of way to the City of Los Angeles with the proviso that the street would be named for him. He also stipulated that the city could not use it for railway lines or for industrial trucking. The area he purchased and developed is now MacArthur Park and the surrounding development of Westlake Park.

In the early 1900s, Wilshire Boulevard was extended to join up with Nevada Avenue in Santa Monica, and the name was changed to Wilshire Boulevard in Santa Monica. Wilshire Boulevard was now sixteen miles from downtown Los Angeles to the ocean at Santa Monica.

Gaylord Wilshire

Gaylord Wilshire was born in Cincinnati, Ohio. He was an avowed and enthusiastic socialist who ran for Congress as a Nationalist Party candidate and for attorney general as the Socialist Labor Party candidate in 1890. His colorful life included running for the Canadian and British Parliaments under the Socialist Party banner. He was also a successful land promoter who developed land in Fullerton, Orange County, and was instrumental in making Long Beach a seaside resort. He gave his name to one of the main thoroughfares of Los Angeles. He was known as the millionaire socialist, publishing a magazine called *Wilshire's Magazine*. George Bernard Shaw, Upton Sinclair and Jack London all wrote for him. His wife was also an active socialist and wrote for his magazine. At one point, the magazine was refused delivery by the U.S. Mail, and Wilshire moved his operations to Canada. Eventually, he returned to Los Angeles and liked to remind everyone that the rapidly expanding boulevard carried his name.

Sunset Boulevard

On its western end, Sunset Boulevard hugs the hills and follows the curves through Bel-Air, Brentwood and Pacific Palisades. Toward the east, the street winds through Beverly Hills, Hollywood and West Hollywood to Olvera Street on its way to Silverlake and Echo Park. In the early part of the twentieth century, this scenic curvy boulevard was called Beverly Drive in West Los Angeles. The paving ran out in Brentwood at the Bristol traffic circle. From there on, it was a rutted dirt road through Brentwood that petered out to an old Chumash trail that led to the ocean. In 1921, Will Rogers bought his estate on the rumor that the road would be paved all the way to the beach. The road was finally paved through to the ocean in 1926.

The name was changed from Beverly Drive to Sunset Boulevard in 1934. The roller coaster aspects of the street were partly caused—according to Wilkie Woodard, the engineer who laid out Bel-Air for A. Bell—by the difficulty in acquiring right of ways. The street has always been busy and dangerous.

There is a great story about Billie Burke, best known for her role as the good witch in *The Wizard of Oz*, who wanted a traffic light installed at Woodburn Drive so that her grandchildren and their friends could run across Sunset

Boulevard to catch their bus to school without risking life and limb. The city hemmed and hawed over the project and finally told Burke that there would have to be three accidents "susceptible to correction by a light" before they would consider adding the light. Rather than sacrifice three children to gain the light, Ms. Burke notified the powers that be that she would be calling the radio, newspapers and TV stations to notify them that she would be directing traffic in her housecoat the following week on Monday morning at eight o'clock. Miraculously, a traffic light appeared before she needed to perform this feat. However, further improvements over the years have been difficult to accomplish, and the road remains congested. Its hairpin curves and speeding commuters continue to take lives.

Highway 1/The Pacific Coast Highway

In West Los Angeles, California Highway 1 has several names—Lincoln Boulevard through Westchester and Marina del Rey; the Santa Monica Freeway; Palisades Beach Road (once called the Roosevelt Highway) in Santa Monica; and finally the Pacific Coast Highway through Pacific Palisades and Malibu. It follows a wandering inland route until it breaks out through the Olympic Tunnel (now McClure Tunnel) to the beach. The Santa Monica Malibu section was started in 1925 and completed in 1929. It was named "Theodore Roosevelt Highway" after the first Roosevelt president. (The section of the road from Carmel to San Simeon was called the Roosevelt Highway after Franklin D. Roosevelt.) In 1932, the cycling events for the 1932 Olympics were held on the section between Oxnard and Santa Monica.

As Santa Monica developed, the road along the beach developed with it. However, the flow of traffic was slowed when it came to expanding the road through Rancho Malibu. May Rindge was successful in keeping the Southern Pacific from crossing her ranch, but having won that battle, she immediately faced a similar battle to prevent the public road from crossing her land. Rindge felt that the ranch was her private property and that the public had no right to access. For many years, the point was moot—few people had any reason to need access to the ranch, and it remained isolated and private.

However, the Rindges improved the primitive trails that had been enough for the original settlers, and the automobile made people more mobile and able to visit the ranch. More people wanted a direct and shorter route to Ventura and Santa Barbara over those roads. The influx of traffic created its own problems. People often camped out on the ranch, and more squatters appeared, resulting in trash and—more seriously—fires and interference with the livestock that was the ranch's main business. Smugglers still used the isolated coves to import liquor, opium and illegal Chinese labor. There were safety concerns. In 1894, to remedy the problems, F. Rindge installed gates on the wagon road and offered keys to his neighbors who needed to use the road. After Rindge's death, fences were installed across the beach roads.

By 1907, the situation had degenerated into a legal fight between both the state and federal governments and May Rindge. The newspapers sided with the homesteaders who wanted access. Rindge was dubbed "the Queen of Malibu" and demonized as the wealthy woman who did not care about her neighbors or their needs. The case took years and was so contentious that

Arch Rock along the coastal road was picturesque, but as automobiles became the norm, it quickly became a hindrance. It collapsed in the middle of the night—either from natural causes or because it was secretly dynamited by those who wanted to widen the road.

a judge had to be imported from Portland to hear the litigation. Eventually (and it took years), the judge decided in Rindge's favor, holding that the public had no right to cross private land to reach public land.

That didn't end the problems, however. The public took its case to Los Angeles County and besieged the supervisors with requests for a public right of way through the property. After a number of hearings, the county condemned the right of way in 1919. Rindge locked her gates at Los Flores Canyon and forced the workers to find someone to open them. Once on the ranch, they were required to walk into the construction site. Despite all the obstructions, delays and Rindge's continued court battle, the county road was finished in 1921. Rindge took her case to the Supreme Court, ultimately losing her battle for good in 1923. When the federal highway finally opened in 1929, twenty-two years had passed since the start of the court cases. Malibu old-timers still call the frequent landslides that close the highway "Rindge's Revengc."

Santa Monica Freeway/San Diego Freeway

The arroyo that runs to the beach through the bluffs was used originally as a cart road for the tar that was brought from the seeps at La Brea for shipment to San Francisco. The arroyo separates the central business district of Santa Monica from Ocean Park. It was bridged in the late 1800s at Fourth Street and Ocean Avenue. The arroyo was used for the Southern Pacific and Pacific Electric tracks from the early 1900s. The Main Street Bridge was added in 1925. In the late 1930s, Olympic Boulevard was routed to the arroyo beneath the Main Street Bridge and through the Olympic Tunnel. Olympic Boulevard was rerouted again when the Santa Monica Freeway (I-10) was built in the arroyo.

The Santa Monica Freeway opened in 1966, linking downtown Los Angeles and Santa Monica. The I-10, as it is officially called, runs east–west from the Arizona border to the beach at Santa Monica, where it pushes through the McClure Tunnel and becomes the Pacific Coast Highway. With its opening, it made the West Side of Los Angeles more accessible to residents who worked in the San Fernando Valley or downtown. Suddenly the beach areas with their smog-free air became even more desirable, and property values soared accordingly.

The Sepulveda Freeway—or, as it is better known, I-405 or the San Diego Freeway—follows the same route as Sepulveda Boulevard from the I-10 in Culver City through the pass into the San Fernando Valley. It bisects

Westwood and Bel-Air from Brentwood and splits Santa Monica along north and south lines. The freeway is heavily traveled by commuters and airport traffic and provides Brentwood, Westwood, Bel-Air and parts of Santa Monica with access to downtown Los Angeles and the Valley.

McClure Tunnel

The tunnel that allows traffic to flow through the bluffs in Santa Monica and onto the Pacific Coast Highway started out as a railroad tunnel for the Southern Pacific and a bridge extending Ocean Avenue over the arroyo into Ocean Park. The railroad constructed the tunnel in order to run trains along the coast to the Long Wharf—the freight pier the Southern Pacific had built north of Santa Monica in its attempt to make Santa Monica Bay the Port of Los Angeles. General Sherman leased the Southern Pacific track for his streetcars and advertised the wharf as an attraction, with the slogan "Ride the rails on the ocean." The tunnel was just below the steps to the beach and the Arcadia Hotel. The wooden bridge/tunnel gave way to a concrete span in 1902.

This bridge/tunnel was demolished when the road was repurposed as part of the Roosevelt Highway. Construction began as a WPA project in 1935,

The McClure Tunnel is the transition at the end of the Santa Monica Freeway—going north it becomes the Pacific Coast Highway with an ocean view. As this photo shows, originally the tunnel brought the Southern Pacific Railroad through the arroyo and under the Ocean Avenue Bridge. The steps to the Arcadia Hotel are visible on the right-hand side of the photograph.

and the Olympic Tunnel opened in 1935. Along with this construction, the Pacific Electric tracks were rerouted and Olympic Boulevard was routed through the tunnel now used for automobiles only. This tunnel is a good example of the WPA Moderne or Deco Moderne architectural style and is consistent with Santa Monica City Hall and the Santa Monica Civic Auditorium nearby.

The tunnel was renamed the Robert E. McClure tunnel in 1969 when it became the terminus for the new I-10 freeway. McClure was the editor and publisher of the *Santa Monica Outlook* and a member of the California Highway Commission. He was instrumental in the effort to extend the freeway system to Santa Monica.

Chapter 5

AMUSEMENTS

It is no surprise that the residents living in the everyday resort environment of West Los Angeles were (and are) avid consumers of all the amusements the area could provide. The weather encouraged an outdoor life, and sports of all kinds became popular. Tennis, golf, polo, swimming, surfing, volleyball, horseback riding and auto races attracted participants and spectators. Without the distractions of television and computers, the early residents amused themselves and built numerous edifices to indulge their pastimes—speedways, polo fields, beach clubs, tennis courts, bridle trails, pools and golf courses.

Piers, Pleasure Parks, Hotels and Bathhouses

West Los Angeles is dominated by the beach. There are over fifty miles of coastline between Malibu and Playa del Rey, much of it accessible to the swimmers, surfers and sun worshipers who join the residents on weekends and holidays. There are twenty-two public beaches. Santa Monica Canyon was one of the earliest beach resorts in Southern California. As early as the 1850s, campers brought tents and sometimes built their own rough cottages along the mouth of the canyon and at the edge of the mesas, enjoying the waves and the canyon's cool creeks and shady trees with little regard for who owned the land.

Surfing became popular here and debuted to the teenage psyches of the 1950s through the songs of the Beach Boys and the Gidget movies; Muscle Beach gave the world bodybuilders like Arnold Schwarzenegger and early gymnasts; pleasure piers thrust into the ocean with all sorts of entertainments;

Venice added canals to the mix; and gambling ships standing three miles offshore provided another layer of entertainment. Over one hundred years of beachgoers have seen it all.

Shoo Fly Landing/ The Long Wharf

The Shoo Fly Landing was the first pier located in the Santa Monica area. It was located at the end of the arroyo (now the Santa Monica Freeway) and was used to ship brea or tar from the tar pits in Los Angeles to San Francisco. The pier was a rough wooden structure located at approximately the end of present-day Colorado Avenue and was built in about 1875. R.S. Baker landed there on his first trip to the Rancho San Vicente y Santa Monica. Senator Jones and Baker built a new pier at the same site as the terminus for their Los Angeles and Independence Railroad. Business was brisk for a few years, with several trains a day and several steamers a week. However, by 1887, the boom was over and the operation was losing money. Jones could not continue to fund it and sold the line and the pier to C.P. Huntington and the Southern Pacific.

After Huntington bought the Los Angeles and Independence Railroad from Jones and Baker in 1877, service was reduced to two steamers a week. In 1879, the Southern Pacific dismantled the Shoo Fly Landing, and Santa Monica was no longer visited by the steamers from San Francisco. In 1893, as part of his efforts to make Santa Monica Bay the Port of Los Angeles, Collis P. Huntington extended the Southern Pacific tracks along the beach and built the Long Wharf at Potrero Canyon (north of Santa Monica Canyon). The pier was one of the longest ever built on the coast and included freight terminals and coaling bunkers for ships. By 1898, Huntington had lost the battle for the port to San Pedro, but the Long Wharf continued to handle freight until it was dismantled in the early 1920s. The heavy timbers from the pier found their way into the Bradbury House built by John Byers in Santa Monica Canyon and to other building projects as far south as San Diego County.

Until they were destroyed, the Southern Pacific tracks along the beach and on the Long Wharf were also used for the Pacific Electric streetcars. As part of the famous Balloon Route, the streetcars trundled down the beach and then onto the pier so that riders could disembark and admire the views across the bay while standing over the water.

Jones and Baker built the Santa Monica Bath House in 1876 on the North Beach near the Ninety-Nine Steps, which provided access from the bluff. It was next to the first bathhouse in the area, built by Patrick Duffy. By 1894, it was considered obsolete, and Sumner Hunt was commissioned to build the North Beach Bathhouse. Its amenities included a saltwater and a freshwater pool, dining rooms, a roof garden and a ballroom. Other attractions were added along the way, including a bowling alley and a plank walk down the beach. One of the attractions was the Camera Obscura that allowed visitors to enjoy 360-degree views of the bay and mountains. (The Camera Obscura survives to this day as part of the Senior Center in Palisades Park. It is free and open for visits.)

In 1877, the Pascual Marquez Beach House was built, also by Patrick Duffy, and named for the Marquez family who owned the land. It was located just north of current Chautauqua Boulevard. Visitors arrived each Sunday by horse-drawn stage from Los Angeles. The route from LA was along present-day Washington Boulevard, then one of the only connecting roads from LA to Santa Monica. The bathhouse improved the canyon's facilities, which up until then had consisted of tents and a small store.

Arcadia Hotel

In 1886, J.W. Scott, who had been the host of the Santa Monica Hotel, the original inn in Santa Monica, purchased a plot of land that he subdivided into forty lots for sale. With the proceeds from the lot sales, he developed a first-class hotel for Santa Monica. The hotel was completed and opened in 1887 and was considered one of the finest on the coast. Scott named his new hotel after Arcadia Bandini de Baker. The Arcadia Hotel included a gravity railroad that brought visitors from the train station and a bathhouse. The hotel had running hot and cold water, electric and gas lights and bathrooms. Its dining rooms boasted shimmering crystal, and its bathhouse was the most "modern" on the coast. Dignitaries visiting the Soldiers Home and prominent Angelenos overnighted at the Arcadia in style. The demise of the Port of Los Angeles idea doomed the hotel, and it was torn down in 1909. Today, the Lowes Santa Monica Beach Hotel sits on its site, and its ballroom is also named for Arcadia Bandini de Stearns de Baker.

Ocean Park

Ocean Park's entertainment history began with the Kenilworth Ostrich Farm, a popular weekend destination, and the Ocean Park Casino. Abbott Kinney and his partner, Francis Ryan, acquired the casino—a restaurant and tennis club—in 1891. They also purchased the surrounding land from W.D. Vawter.

This Ocean Park logo seems to describe the whole development—homes, amusement pier and the Pacific Ocean—in one lighthearted drawing.

Some of the plot was part of the Rancho La Ballona. The northern part of the land was buildable, but the southern portion was salt marsh.

When the Southern Pacific was unwilling to extend its line into the area, Kinney made a deal with the Santa Fe Railroad. The Santa Fe had extended a line to the port at Rancho La Ballona Lagoon during its failed dredging operation. It agreed to extend its line from there to Ocean Park. The first train arrived in 1892, bringing tourists for the growing group of attractions that Kinney and his partners were adding to Ocean Park. In 1898, Santa Monica gave Kinney and Ryan permission to build a pier on the pilings that were already carrying the city's sewer pipes out to sea. The pier was for walking and fishing but did not have any other entertainment attractions. Kinney built a racetrack and golf links as part of his Casino Country Club at about the same time.

Kinney took ownership of the salt marshes and left Ocean Park to his partners on the toss of a coin in 1904. His former partners continued to develop the area around the pier into "the Coney Island of the Pacific." They added the Ocean Park Plunge, an ornate indoor saltwater swimming pool, and a number of other attractions, including the Ocean Park Bath House—a Byzantine confection of minarets and domes. Gradually, attractions were added to the piers themselves—rides, games, restaurants, ballrooms and theaters all came and went on the piers.

Other piers were added or replaced piers that were destroyed by fire and storms—Horseshoe Pier, Marine Pier and the Million Dollar Pier. Three piers replaced the Million Dollar Pier after it burned, one with a "mountain

Tourists promenade along busy Pier Avenue in Ocean Park. The casino is on the left.

roll" or roller coaster. Successive piers included the Lick Pier, with its popular Aragon Ballroom, and Ocean Park Pier. Ocean Park Pier became Pacific Ocean Park (POP) in 1958, an attempt to compete with Disneyland's increasing popularity. POP was said to stand for "Pay One Price—Play all Day," an obvious contrast to Disneyland's now gone ticket system. POP never could outdo Disneyland, and after years of losing money, it burned down in 1974. It has been replaced by high-rise condo buildings and hotels, ending Ocean Park's Coney Island vibe.

Playa del Rey

Competing with Ocean Park was another development farther south on the Rancho La Ballona. Playa del Rey was the project of General Sherman and a syndicate of investors, including Arthur Fleming, R.C. Gillis and other prominent Santa Monica businessmen. The Beach Land Company

Playa del Rey was a popular stop on the Balloon Route once Sherman and Clark built their auditorium and other attractions. This postcard was sent in 1908. The sender did not go to Playa del Rey but mentioned that it was near Venice Beach, indicating the prominence that Venice Beach was beginning to assert over both Ocean Beach and Playa del Rey.

began its development in 1902 and at first planned an ambitious layout along the lines of Venice, Italy, called Playa del Rey. The costs of such an undertaking quickly lowered expectations, and eventually the development comprised a hotel, a pier and a wooden speedway for auto races. Sherman quickly extended his streetcars to the area, and soon thousands of visitors were flocking into the area each weekend. Lack of funds, fire and storms eventually wiped out the pier, and the other attractions were eclipsed by Venice and Ocean Park.

Venice Beach

In 1904, Abbott Kinney, having secured property with a natural source of water, set out to develop his vision of Venice of America on the beach in California. When he opened his new beachfront property in 1905, he had dug several miles of canals to drain the marshes and form the centerpieces of his new city. He had constructed a 1,400-foot pier that included among its attractions an auditorium, a hot saltwater plunge, the Ship Restaurant and a dance hall. The pier was accompanied by an arcaded Italianate block of shops. Visitors rode the Red Cars to Santa Monica and then took

The Italianate buildings and wide steps contribute to the exotic atmosphere created at Venice Beach. Postcards such as these were often sent as a "wish you were here" note to relatives back home in order to entice them to move to California.

a miniature railroad to Venice, as it officially became known in 1911. They rode in gondolas to explore the town. More and more attractions were added to the Kinney Pier for the amusement of its visitors—an aquarium, rides like the Virginia Reel and the Racing Derby, restaurants and game booths. The pier burned in 1920, six weeks after Kinney's death, but the family quickly rebuilt a bigger and better pier. It opened on Memorial Day in 1921 with two roller coasters, a new Racing Derby and much more. In 1925, a third coaster was added, along with a fun house and a flying circus aerial ride. Several hundred thousand tourists descended on the pier every weekend.

Venice was annexed to the City of Los Angeles in 1925 and immediately ran afoul of the city's "blue laws." No dancing on Sunday and no gambling games sent visitors to nearby Ocean Park in Santa Monica. The citizens of Venice circulated a petition to establish an amusement zone on their pier. Enough signatures were gathered to force an election in 1926. The city voters agreed with the Venice residents, and the pier was allowed to resume business as usual in May 1926. With the Depression, the pier began to deteriorate. Attendance and spending dropped, maintenance was delayed and, in 1932, the Kinney Company defaulted on its bonds. The company went into bankruptcy, but the pier struggled on through the rest of the Depression and World War II. After the war, however, the city surprised everyone when it refused to renew the Kinney Company's lease. The pier closed for good on April 20, 1946. Most of the rides went to other parks, the buildings were demolished and a fire finished off the rest of the pier. There is currently a fishing pier in Venice but no pleasure pier.

Santa Monica Pier

The Santa Monica Municipal Pier was built in 1909 at the end of Colorado Boulevard and was the first concrete pier on the coast. The pier did double duty as the conduit that took the city sewer pipes beyond the breakers and provided a promenade for strollers but no other attractions. The concrete pier proved unstable and succumbed to the elements in 1920. It was replaced by the current wooden pier.

Charles Looff, who had developed the real Coney Island, built the Pleasure Pier in 1917 next to the Municipal Pier. The attractions included a roller coaster called the Blue Streak, a swing ride and a bowling and billiard facility. The Hippodrome Carousel Building housed the merry-go-round on the east side of the pier. In 1924, the La Monica Ballroom joined the other attractions. Looff himself carved the first merry-go-round horses.

After several other owners, the Pleasure Pier was acquired by the city in 1953. In 1973, the city decided to remove the piers and replace them with a park. (Ironically, that same year, the pier was featured in the movie *The Sting*.) The community outcry and its ability to organize saved the pier. Today, the pier is a thriving group of rides, restaurants, shops and a restored merry-go-round. It is also the only remaining pleasure pier left on the California coast.

Rile

One of the attractions on the beach in Santa Monica was the H.F. Rile Photographic Studio, where beachgoers could stop and have a picture taken. Harry Frantz Rile arrived in Santa Monica in about 1877 and opened his studio in North Beach. Rile was from Pennsylvania and learned photography in Philadelphia. He worked in Chicago,

This is the back of a photo taken at the Santa Monica Pier. Rile was a clever self-promoter who made sure that anyone who had their picture taken in his studio would continue advertising his business as they showed the photograph to friends.

Kansas City, Portland and San Francisco before coming to Santa Monica. Rile's photos were done in the style of carte de visites—small photographs mounted on 2.5- by 4-inch cards. Rile's advertising was on the back, and he became known far and wide as the cards were sent to relatives and friends. They were easy to mail and did not require special handling. They were also inexpensive—the perfect souvenir of a day spent at the beach. Many of the early photos of Santa Monica are attributed to Rile.

Balloon Route

The Los Angeles Pacific operated Balloon Route excursions early on, but they did not become a popular phenomenon until C.M. Pierce took over the management and publicity of the sightseeing trolley trip in 1904. Pierce assembled guides, printed circulars, distributed them to all the hotels in Los Angeles and added a photographer. The first stop on the trip was an artist's studio in Hollywood. The next was the Old Soldiers Home, where passengers lined up on the dining room steps for a picture. The photographer would then take the film downtown on another trolley for development.

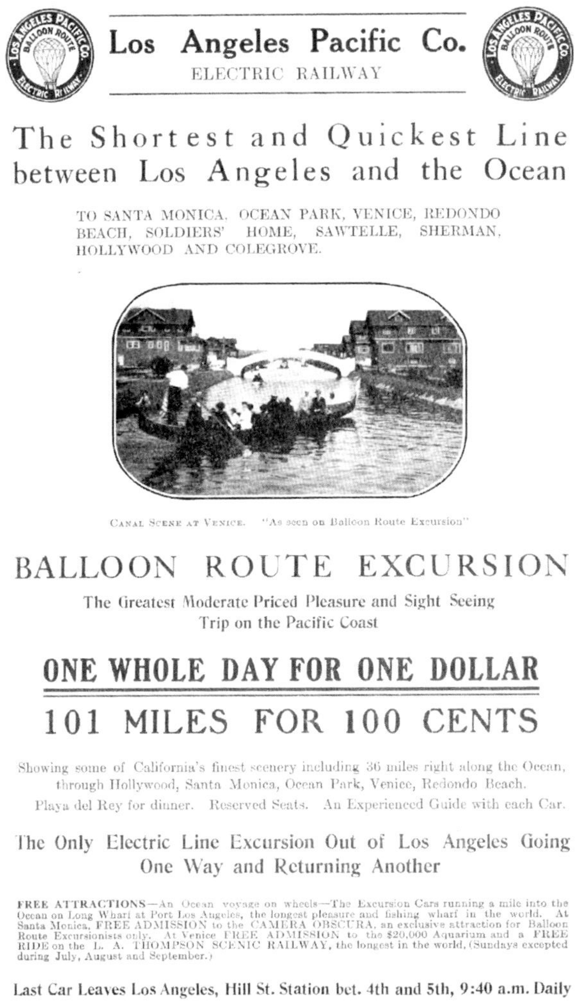

The Balloon Route was the ultimate ticket for Angelenos in the early part of the twentieth century. Riders paid their fare in Hollywood and then rode all day for one dollar. The route took them to the Soldiers Home, where they posed for pictures; to the Long Wharf, where they marveled at the views; through Venice; and to Playa del Rey for a catered lunch. When they returned to their starting point, their photographs would be waiting for them.

Trolley riders picked up their pictures at the end of the tour—very much like today's amusement park photos. The next stop was the Long Wharf, then the Camera Obscura in Santa Monica. A fish luncheon was served at the Playa del Rey Pavilion. For a small fee, riders could also use the skating rink or take a boat ride. From there, the trolley went to Redondo Beach, and the passengers were allowed to scour Moonstone Beach for specimens of moonstones. Then it was back to Venice so that passengers could survey the canals and the pier. The return trip was through Palms.

The scenic trip cost one dollar, and passengers were given a 101-mile trip for their hundred pennies. They saw 36 miles of coastline and many attractions during their day on the trolley. It was by far the most famous of the trolley sightseeing runs. It also served as advertising for the growing towns and neighborhoods of the Westside.

Automobile Races

Streetcars dominated West Los Angeles transportation in the early days of the twentieth century, and horses were still an important part of life, but residents were already turning to automobiles for work and sport. Gillis bought a Locomobile in 1906 for $5,000, having been assured that it was the best in the world. C.L. Bundy and L.D. Loomis tooled around the Westgate construction site in a Cartercar or a Winton Touring Car. Traffic may not have been heavy, but residents were already turning barns into garages and turning their carriage horses out to pasture. The enthusiasm for automobiles extended to racing them for sport.

Los Angeles Motordrome

The Los Angeles Motordrome was built in 1910 in Playa del Rey. It was an all-wooden speedway with a one-mile circular track based on a French velodrome, and in its day, it rivaled the Indianapolis Speedway. It was a project of Frank A. Garbutt and a syndicate of automobile racing enthusiasts. The site was chosen because of its proximity to Garbutt's home, built in Sherman and Clark's Beach Land Company Playa del Rey development. Called the "pie pan," the track was made up of thousands of two- by four-inch boards, and it was very fast and extremely dangerous. There were a number of fatalities over its time of operation. Barney Oldfield was able to do a record ninety-nine miles per hour on it soon after it opened. It was located near

Speedway Boulevard (now Culver Boulevard)—so named because it was one of the first paved roads in Los Angeles and was its fastest straightaway. The motordrome attracted visitors and racing enthusiasts. It was also the site of bicycle and motorcycle races and air shows. In 1913, the motordrome was destroyed by a fire, ending its three-year run.

Santa Monica Road Races and the Vanderbilt Cup

Given the level of interest in the newfangled machines, several Santa Monica automobile dealers thought it would be a good advertising move to sponsor road races over recently completed Ocean Avenue and Nevada and San Vicente Boulevards. The newly formed Auto Dealers Association of Southern California began looking for a site. One possibility was in the San Fernando Valley, and the other was in Santa Monica. After a heated debate, Santa Monica won the race thanks to its well-oiled roads, sidewalks and resort atmosphere.

The first races in 1909 were local cars and drivers (enforced by a residency requirement) going as fast as possible around an approximately eight-mile course. The total race was two hundred miles and twenty-four laps. Automobiles started on Ocean Avenue near Montana Avenue, went south along Ocean Avenue to Nevada Avenue making a tight ninety-degree left-hand turn, soon to be nicknamed "Deadman's Curve," into a three-mile

Road racing was a popular sport when automobiles were new, and top speeds were approaching sixty miles per hour. Bruce Brown was a well-liked driver in the 1912 Santa Monica Road race, although he did not win. He was killed in another race several months later and much mourned in Santa Monica.

straightaway. Another left-hand turn at the Soldiers Home took the autos onto San Vicente Boulevard and back to the start line. Three dealers made up the rules for the new sport. The goal of the race was to promote Santa Monica and sell automobiles. The race was run with stock cars—there were few race cars located on the West Coast at the time. The cars included an Apperson Jackrabbit, a Locomobile, a Lozier, a Haynes, a Studebaker, a Pope-Hartford and many others.

Grandstands were built at Ocean Boulevard and the Soldiers Home. There were plenty of vacant lots and homes with second stories along the route that could be used for viewing. Some homeowners built their own viewing stands. Each car had its pit and group of rooters. The *Los Angeles Times* ran contests for readers to guess the winners and their times. The crowd was estimated at fifty thousand. Harris Hanshue in his Apperson Jackrabbit won the heavy car race, and Bett Dingley in a Chalmers-Detroit won the light car race.

The sponsors were pleased—no drivers or spectators were injured, and speeds were over sixty miles per hour. They were so pleased that they continued to run races in 1910, 1911 and 1912. Each of the three races pulled over 100,000 people to Santa Monica to watch the racers. They also pulled in drivers like Barney Oldfield and Ralph De Palma with national reputations and records. By 1913, though, the races were faced with conflicts among the organizers and did not have as many of the top drivers. Automobiles were no longer novelties, and the races were losing their impact as sales tools. Some thought the day of the Santa Monica Road Races was done, but 1914 turned out to be the best year yet.

The Vanderbilt Cup Race was the premier road race of the day and one of the oldest contests in the country. William Vanderbilt II founded the race in 1904. He offered a sizable purse to attract the best American and European drivers and cars. His goal was to encourage American car manufacturers to produce bigger cars. The first two races attracted large crowds and featured an international field of cars. The 1904, 1905 and 1906 races were won by European drivers. However, after a spectator was killed in 1906, further races were cancelled. Vanderbilt didn't give up though. He formed a company and built a multimillion-dollar toll road to be used for the race and also opened it for public use. It was the first concrete auto highway in the world. Once the road was finished, the race resumed in 1908. To the delight of the crowd, a Locomobile driven by American George Robinson won the race. (The car still exists and is located at the Henry Ford Museum in Dearborn, Michigan.)

The races moved to Savannah and Milwaukee in succeeding years, but Vanderbilt was not satisfied with either venue and decided instead to bring his race to Santa Monica. Now Santa Monica had a chance for the best drivers, the best cars and national attention. The course was improved, and once again, rivals Barney Oldfield and Ralph De Palma signed on to race. So did Eddie Rickenbacker. However, February is right in the middle of the rainy season, and the rains started on the Tuesday before the Saturday race. After a three-day deluge, the roads from Los Angeles were mired in mud, and the prospects for spectators were diminished. The race was postponed until the next week. Once the ground dried out, the race was a spectacular event. Oldfield and De Palma dueled the whole race, with De Palma eventually winning. Over 100,000 people watched the race, and numerous reporters and photographers covered the story for the national press.

The next year, the Vanderbilt Cup was wooed to San Francisco to take part in the Panama Pacific International Exposition, but it returned to Santa Monica in 1916. In the interim, Ocean Avenue had been paved, speeding up the course. Speeds over one hundred miles per hour were possible. For the first time since the Santa Monica races started, a major accident during practice killed a driver, a woman running a lemonade stand, a spectator and a photographer. Though the event was still considered successful, the fatal crash dimmed the luster of road racing in general, and the American entry in World War I contributed to ending the races for the next few years. One final race was held in 1919, but the increasing population in Santa Monica—it had doubled since 1909—the advanced speeds of the cars and the death of a driver doomed Santa Monica's street racing days.

The Vanderbilt Cup put Santa Monica on the national map and lifted it beyond sleepy resort status to a mature city. In a very real sense, it made it possible for the city to remain independent of its major neighbor, Los Angeles. It also accomplished its goal of increasing automobile sales.

Beach Clubs

During the Roaring Twenties, beach clubs became a popular diversion for Angelenos. From 1915 to 1920, sixteen private, members-only clubs were built along the Santa Monica Beach. The clubs were either branches of the downtown clubs, like the Jonathan Club and the Santa Monica Athletic Club; founded by groups of friends who were united by a love of the beach, in the case of The Beach Club; created by real estate developers, like the Bel-Air Bay Club; or created by commercial interests, like the Edgewater, the Waverly and the Deauville. Some of the clubs were big enough to function as hotels for their members. Several other clubs were planned and in construction when the Depression derailed their plans, and they were never finished. At first, the clubs only operated in the summer and were often havens for residents of Pasadena and other summer hot spots. Gradually they became year-round facilities, and the five that are left have full-time staffs and programs. (Rumors always flew that the clubs also provided slot machines for their members to do a little discreet gambling.)

The clubs that sprang up during the 1920s were: the Santa Monica Athletic Club, demolished in the 1950s; the Santa Monica Swimming Club, demolished in 1955; the Breakers, converted to apartments; the Bel-Air Bay Club, still thriving; the Miramar Beach Club, demolished in the early '50s; The Beach Club, still open; Casa Del Mar, converted to a hotel; the Sorrento Beach Club, destroyed by fire; the Jonathan Club, still open; the Saltair Club (nicknamed the Dirty Thirties), still open; the Edgewater and the Waverly, torn down and now the sites of Shutters and At the Beach; the Deauville, demolished in 1966; and the Palisades Beach Club (usually called the Filthy Fifties), still open.

The Beach Club

Founded in 1923 by a group of like-minded beach lovers, The Beach Club is well known for its wide beach and colorful umbrellas. The group banded together to purchase beach frontage and construct facilities for their families, becoming one of the first two private clubs on the beach.

The beaches provided surf and fun for residents and tourists alike. Cabanas provided changing facilities and a place to hang bathing suits to dry. Beach clothes were almost as formal as street clothes for both women and children, including shoes and hats.

Duke Kahanamoku was hired as the athletic director and lifeguard in 1925 and introduced the members to both surfing and beach volleyball. He is credited with evolving the beach volleyball game from a leisurely sport to a more athletic one. He was famous for fabulous jumps and wicked spikes. The Beach Club's volleyball teams were well known and competed in both state and national contexts. Many high school and college players learned the game at The Beach Club and went on to play in high school and college. Other activities included paddle tennis and youth groups for members' children during the summer. Social events and dining were also part of the member activities.

In 1954, the Santa Monica Swimming Club next door (founded by a group of movie industry people) went up for sale, and The Beach Club bought the property, demolished the clubhouse and built a 250-space parking lot, solving their parking problem.

Bel-Air Bay Club

Alphonzo Bell decided to build a beach club on the sixty-seven acres he purchased from the Santa Monica Mountain Park Company (SMMPC) near the mouth of Santa Inez Canyon above the new Pacific Coast Highway. In typical Bell fashion, he planned an extensive facility—homes and a beach club that would be "A Country Place by the Sea." Utilities were to be underground, and lots were sited to preserve views and privacy. Italian names were given to the winding streets. The land included 900 feet of shoreline, but there was little beach. Fortunately for Bell, Wilkie Woodard, his engineer and the engineer for the Santa Monica Mountain Park Company (and a number of other Gillis and Bell projects), created a system of groins for the shoreline in order to build up the sand for the SMMPC. Over the years, the groins extended Bell's beach frontage by 300 feet, making a "beach" club possible. They continue to protect the club's shoreline frontage and have been added to and made more permanent over the years. Later, another 360 feet were added to the shore frontage, giving the club 1,200 feet altogether.

With his sand ensured, Bell turned to Elmer Grey and Grey's partner Mark Daniels to design Upper and Lower Clubhouses. The Upper Club was to be a formal facility with oversized fireplaces, thirteen bedrooms, a 360-degree view of the coastline and mountains, a pool, tennis courts and fifteen casitas. The Lower Club was to be built quickly in order to be open while the other facilities were being built. The project was incorporated in 1927 with Bell as president, R.C. Gillis as first vice-president and several

The Bel-Air Bay Club's Upper Club sits on its hill overlooking the coast above its Lower Club on the sand. The groins are clearly visible and have already built the sand up into a reasonable beach in this picture taken in the 1940s.

other prominent businessmen as the rest of the board. While the charter allowed for six hundred members, there were twenty-nine members on opening day when the Lower Club opened with a small pavilion for parties, dressing rooms and a grill.

Construction began on the Upper Club in 1929 with a projected cost of $200,000. Unfortunately for Bell's grand plans, the Depression hit about the same time construction started. Plans were scaled back, and the final club did not include the pools, underground garage, tennis courts, stables or elevator. The tower, planned as Bell's office, remained hollow and unfinished. The Upper Club opened in 1931 and even in its reduced layout quickly established itself as an elegant facility for parties, weddings and other celebrations. Even after several renovations, it remains very close to Bell's original vision of what a private club should look like.

The Lower Club has always featured cabanas for members that were often second homes during the summer for those who lived in Pasadena or other inland areas. Badminton courts were the first sports facilities at the Lower Club. Surfing and paddleboards were also popular by the

'30s. Paddle tennis was introduced in 1938. The club rapidly developed a reputation for that sport, and the Bel-Air Bay Club teams have earned many trophies and championships over the years. Volleyball became popular in the 1940s, and many players trained there have won distinction in high school, college and other competitions. The Coach Group for the children of members was (and is) a five-day-a-week summer program that teaches swimming, crafts and all kinds of games. Its graduates never forget their summer days on the beach in the care of college-aged counselors. The Lower Club has also been renovated many times—sometimes by the ocean, sometimes by design. Its most recent reincarnation maintains its charm but has added many amenities

In order to jumpstart his residential subdivision, Bell gave a prime lot to a friend with the proviso that he build a showplace that would help sell his other lots. The Castle was designed by Paul Williams and finished in 1931. It was the only house in the subdivision for a number of years, but after World War II, the area filled up with the homes that matched Bell's vision.

The Bel-Air Bay Club is reputed to be the setting for Raymond Chandler's Belvedere Beach Club in *Farewell My Lovely*. His description of the overgrown lots and the club sitting among the brush rings true for the time frame of the novel.

Jonathan Club

The Jonathan Club was founded in 1895 by a group of men who were part of a Los Angeles marching society. The club has its own building in downtown Los Angeles on Figueroa Street and counts many distinguished Angelenos as its members—H.E. Huntington was a founder. The club's Santa Monica location on the beach near the California Incline opened in 1927 as the Sea Breeze Beach Club. The Jonathan Club Beach took it over in 1933. The club leases some of its beachfront from the City of Santa Monica (recently reluctantly renewed by Santa Monica, which was under pressure to make the beach public). The downtown club was an all-white male bastion until the late 1980s (as were all the clubs), when Los Angeles passed an ordinance banning discrimination—the first female and African American members were admitted in 1987. The Santa Monica facility was also restricted for race and religion until the late 1980s. Members of the Jonathan Club Town (the downtown club) can opt to join the Jonathan Club Beach if they so desire. The club is known for its distinctive teal-colored umbrellas and its impressive facilities.

Built in 1927, the Deauville Beach Club looks more like a French chateau than a California bathhouse.

Other Clubs

The Deauville was built on the site of the old North Beach Bathhouse. The Los Angeles Athletic Club purchased it in 1927 to use as its beach facility. It was designed to look like a French chateau but looked strangely out of place on a California beach. However, it was generally conceded to be the most beautiful of the beach clubs until it burned in the 1950s. The Casa del Mar and the Edgewater were built next door to each other south of the Santa Monica Municipal Pier. The Edgewater was replaced by the Shutters on the Beach Hotel. It was designed to look and feel like the great beach club it replaced. The Casa del Mar remains as a hotel. The Breakers Beach Club was built near the Edgewater and opened in 1928. It reopened in 1934 as the Grand Hotel. It went through many transformations and names until it was badly damaged in the 1994 Northridge earthquake and torn down.

Country Clubs

For those who were not in the mood for beach activities, a number of country clubs were organized in West Los Angeles to cater to residents' love of golf, tennis and polo. The clubs often started as a way to attract buyers to the areas that the capitalists were subdividing. They promised lot buyers a way to amuse themselves, relaxation and a way to enjoy the benefits of living so far from Los Angeles in congenial company.

Los Angeles Country Club

It was really "country" when the founding members of the Los Angeles Golf Club found their permanent home in 1899. The Los Angeles Golf Club was started in 1897 and had already outgrown several sites when Joe Sartori and Ed Tufts found the land that would become the Los Angeles Country Club. The final and permanent permutation of the club was situated in Beverly Hills and opened in 1911. Golfers coming from Los Angeles either drove in their new cars (or buggies) over dusty Wilshire Boulevard or lugged their clubs onto the westbound Pacific Electric trolley at dawn for the trip out to the club. If they were lucky, the club's supply wagon would be at the corner of Wilshire and Santa Monica Boulevards and would give them a ride to

The Los Angeles Country Club sits in the middle of nowhere in 1913. The road is still unpaved, and the water tower dominates the landscape.

the clubhouse. If the wagon was not there, members would raise a flag, and the wagon would wend its way down the hill to pick them up. The road to the club was unpaved, and no doubt the tee times needed to be flexible. The course was rustic at best, cut out of the barley fields, and the third hole was actually across Wilshire Boulevard. Fortunately, traffic was light. Eventually the club laid out two courses with Wilshire Boulevard as the divider.

The club survived its early primitive days to become one of the premier clubs in Los Angeles, with two internationally known golf courses, tennis courts and an elegant clubhouse. The recently renovated North Course is considered one of the top ten in the country. It was originally designed by George Thomas Jr., who also designed the Bel-Air Country Club course and the Riviera Country Club's course. Interestingly, Thomas designed all three courses as a hobby, never accepting a fee. The Los Angeles Country Club design takes full advantage of the hilly terrain to create a challenging course. Many of the homes in Holmby Hills and Beverly Hills back up to the course, including the Playboy Mansion and the huge home of the late Aaron Spelling. It is one of the most private clubs in the city, jealously protecting its members' privacy with guards, a no-cellphone policy and a large membership fee.

Brentwood Country Club

The Brentwood Country Club also had several locations in its early days. Originally it was located on the north side of San Vicente but moved to its current location in the 1920s. The area was originally scheduled to be subdivided as Brentwood Terrace, but sales lagged and the club purchased the property. The site forms a green heart for Brentwood that was almost lost in the late 1940s when it was nearly sold for development. Its outer perimeter is a popular jogging track for locals.

Bel-Air Country Club

Alphonzo Bell's plan for Bel-Air Estates included a world-class country club and golf course. George Thomas Jr. designed the course in 1925. The club's course overlooks Westwood and is considered one of the state's top courses. Bell landscaped the golf course and club in the same lavish style he used in the rest of the subdivision. The course runs through four canyons and includes bridges and tunnels as necessary to traverse the terrain. There is even an elevator and a miniature suspension bridge.

Originally, Bell discouraged the movie crowd from joining the club, but its membership now reads like an industry who's who. Prominent businessmen have also made the club home. Supposedly Howard Hughes, late for a tee time with Katherine Hepburn, landed his plane on the fairway near the fourteenth hole. When the club presented him a bill for its removal, he refused to pay and resigned his membership.

Bell subsidized both the Bel-Air Country Club and the Bel-Air Bay Club by paying operating costs and holding their mortgages. Both clubs were sold to their memberships in the 1940s.

Riviera Club

In the 1920s, the Los Angeles Athletic Club was searching for a golf course and polo field site. Bell offered the group land from his Santa Monica Mountain Park property if the club would build a golf course there. Frank A. Garbutt, head of the club, agreed and helped Bell put together a syndicate to develop the new club and the surrounding land. The land Bell donated is located in Santa Monica Canyon south of Sunset Boulevard. The course was designed by George Thomas Jr. (before he worked on the Los Angeles Country Club courses). The canyon site was difficult to lay out, and it took over fifteen months to finalize the plan. After eighteen months of construction, the course opened in 1927. It cost over $200,000 to construct and at the time was the second-most expensive course in the world. Native trees and streams were preserved as features on the course, including the *barranca* (ravine) that forms a natural hazard. The course fairways are planted with kikuyu grass that supposedly migrated from the club's polo fields. It was also planted after the 1938 flood to hold the wall of the barranca that cuts across the course. It forms one of the thickest roughs in the game. The clubhouse was designed by J. Bernard Richards and opened in 1928.

Douglas Fairbanks and Mary Pickford were early members and promoted the club with offerings of large purses for winning low scores. The Los Angeles Junior Chamber of Commerce picked the club to host the Los Angeles Open in 1929. The club has hosted it ever since. Many famous golfers have won the tournament, including Ben Hogan, who won it three times and also won the United States Open at the club, giving the course its nickname of "Hogan's Alley." Surprisingly, Tiger Woods has never won the Los Angeles Open. Many movies have been filmed on the course, often with famous golfers like Bing Crosby playing cameos.

Uplifters

Members of the Los Angeles Athletic Club formed the Uplifters Club in 1913 to exploit their creative instincts. The name refers to their desire to "uplift" their spirits both literally and figuratively. George Haldeman and L. Frank Baum, author of *The Wizard of Oz* series, were its founding leaders. The group sponsored professional artists and also performed elaborate plays and productions starring their members. One of their events was an annual outing every summer away from the city—sites included the Del Coronado in San Diego, Arrowhead and Big Bear. In 1920, their dream was to find a permanent site for these meetings, and they eventually found property in Rustic Canyon that would fit their needs. The land was originally the Forestry Station established by Abbott Kinney and another piece of property that belonged to George Edmunds and his first wife, a cousin of Frances Gillis.

The Edmunds home became the clubhouse for their celebrations until it burned in 1922. The group built a new headquarters and dedicated it in 1923. A polo field and equestrian facilities were added, with Snowy Baker handling the activities. Guy Bundy led paper chase events (a trail ride with optional jumps that follows a paper trail instead of a fox) through the hills and sometimes played the fox. Eventually, a pool and other amenities were also added. Members built second homes on or near the property. Many of these were log cabins or made to look like log cabins. Will Rogers was a member in good standing, along with Leo Carrillo and many other luminaries from the business and movie worlds. During Prohibition, the club was known as a good place to find a drink. After the Depression and World War II, the club gradually sold off much of its land and disbanded altogether in the 1950s. Its headquarters became Rustic Canyon Park.

Sports and Games

Surfing

It is hard to imagine Santa Monica Bay and West Los Angeles without surfing and all that comes with it: the boards in the water, the bleached-blonde kids, the slang, the "Woodies" and the Beach Boys. However, surfing wasn't a big deal on Westside beaches until the early 1900s—the exact date is murky. George Freeth is generally credited with bringing the sport from Hawaii to the West Coast, although three Hawaiian princes in school in San

Mateo were seen surfing in Santa Cruz in 1885. Freeth was part Hawaiian and part Irish, and in 1907, Jack London wrote a glowing article about his skills riding the waves. Henry E. Huntington read the article and invited Freeth to put on a surfing demonstration as a promotion for his railroad.

Earlier in the century, Abbott Kinney had organized a trained lifeguard service to protect Venice Beach visitors from drowning. Stories about sea rescues from near death were common in the papers, so it seems to have been needed. As well as introducing surfing, Freeth is credited with teaching many of these lifeguards modern techniques for rescuing swimmers. Duke Kahanamoku made a stop in Southern California on his way to the 1912 Olympics and demonstrated his surfing skills for the beachgoers. After that, surfing caught on—first with the heavy 114-pound koa boards that are used in Hawaii and then with lighter and shorter boards pioneered by Tom Blake. In the 1930s, Blake used the Hawaiian boards as a model and patented a lighter hollow board. It became the first production surfboard in the world. The surfboard has been used as one of the lifeguard's primary rescue tools since "The Duke" used his surfboard to rescue a number of men from a sinking fishing boat off Newport Beach.

During the 1920s, Duke Kahanamoku was athletic director and lifeguard for The Beach Club. There he taught surfing and is also credited with introducing beach volleyball to the Santa Monica beach scene.

Surfing's popularity increased during the Depression and really burgeoned after World War II. The 1950s brought more residents to the Westside, and the kids rapidly discovered surfing as a sport. They surfed all of the breaks on Santa Monica Bay. Malibu became known as the best spot, and the surfers quickly figured out how to climb under the fences to surf their favorite break at Malibu Creek. The beach became famous as Surfrider Beach—now Malibu Lagoon State Beach (also the site of the Adamson House Museum). Their rapidly evolving culture took over the beach and the whole of Southern California. Soon everyone knew a "gremlin" from a "hodad"; Mom's uncool wood-trimmed station wagon was suddenly a status symbol; and peroxide and sun were the hair dyes of choice. After Brentwood resident Frederick Kohner published his first Gidget book in 1957—based on his daughter Kathy's surfing adventures—surfing became a "cool" California thing for the rest of the country. (Kathy Zuckerman, the "girl midget" who hung out at Malibu, still lives on the Westside and surfs occasionally for charity.)

Segregated beaches were the norm in West Los Angeles until the 1940s, even though they were officially made illegal in 1927. Inkwell Beach at the foot of Pico Boulevard was the place for African Americans in Santa

Surfing USA. The surfboards started out taller than the surfers, but it didn't hinder the sport as it developed on the beaches of the Westside.

Monica during the 1920s. The site was once the Crystal Plunge, a swimming pool that was destroyed by a flood in 1905. One of the most famous Santa Monica surfers learned the sport at Inkwell and became the first known black surfer. Nat Gabaldon was taught to surf as a teenager by the legendary Santa Monica lifeguard Pete Peterson, and when Gabaldon returned from his stint in the navy in 1946, he became known for his surfing prowess. He was a fixture at Surfrider Beach in Malibu and part of the legendary group that hung out there until his death surfing a ten-foot wave in 1951.

Horses and Polo

Horses and horse activities were an integral part of West Los Angeles until World War I. First for transportation: the children rode their ponies to school; horse-drawn equipment dragged the roads before they were paved; businessmen went to work in runabouts; and horses pulled the streetcars. Gradually the horses gave way to the newfangled motorcars and electric trolleys. Recreation with horses became more important than transportation.

Adelaide Gillis riding her prizewinning Kentucky American Saddlebred horse, Don Costanio. He was trained at the San Vicente stable in Sullivan Canyon. The stable was the center for Adelaide Gillis McCormick's horse training business in the 1930s.

R.C. Gillis built a stable at the mouth of Sullivan Canyon (north of Sunset Boulevard) for his daughter's horses. Adelaide Gillis was an avid horsewoman, and she lobbied her father unmercifully for a pony and cart as a young child and training horses as she grew older. Her father purchased a Kentucky American Saddlebred horse for her to train. Don Costanio thrived in Sullivan Canyon and won best horse at the California State Fair in 1912.

The Riviera developed the Riviera Polo Club and Equestrian Center south of Sunset Boulevard at the mouth of Sullivan Canyon. The facilities included stables that could house 350 horses, a training track, a steeplechase course and three polo fields. Snowy Baker managed the equestrian facilities, and the club was soon famous both for the riders who trained there—Elizabeth Taylor learned to ride here for her part in *National Velvet*—and the famous people who played polo there. The Riviera Riders, many of them movie stars, cantered over fifty miles of trails that led over the hills and canyons as yet untouched by subdivisions.

The facility hosted the equestrian events of the 1932 Los Angeles Olympics. Twenty thousand residents and visitors enjoyed boxes along the polo field, sat in the grandstand or scrambled up into the hills to watch while the cavalries of the world competed. Baron Takeichi Nishi of Japan was very popular and won a gold medal for Japan. (He would die defending the island of Iwo Jima from the Americans some thirteen years later.) It remains the only gold medal ever won by the Japanese in equestrian events. Dorothy Gillis Loomis, who lived in the Dutch East Indies with her first husband, entertained the Dutch team during the competition.

Polo was introduced to West Los Angeles by the members of the colony of English expats living in Santa Monica. The first match was played in 1878, and the English lost to Manuel Marquez and his vaqueros. The English persevered, however, and formed the California Polo Club. In 1889, Jones and Baker donated land for a field—the site of today's Christine Reed Park. Matches were held there on Wednesdays and Saturdays and were the occasion for picnics, teas, parties and gala balls. Spectators who often drove out from Los Angeles were amused by the sight of the players filling gopher holes before each match.

With five polo fields in the neighborhood, Sullivan, Mandeville and Rustic Canyons were home to a number of well-known polo strings and riders, including Elizabeth Whitney and C.D. LeBlanc. Their horses were stabled close enough to walk over to the fields for practice and games. The Beverly Hills Polo Club played there every Sunday during the season. A women's team also played matches.

Will Rogers was a polo enthusiast and purchased a ranch in the same area, constructing a polo field before he even finished his home. Pick-up polo matches were often held there on Sunday mornings with his famous friends making up the teams. Some of the celebrities who played with him included David Niven, Spencer Tracy, Walt Disney and Clark Gable.

In the 1950s, the Riviera's polo fields were sold to the Los Angeles Board of Education for the construction of a middle school. Paul Revere Junior High School opened in 1955. The other fields were gradually subdivided. The only remaining polo field is the one on Will Rogers's ranch. It still hosts polo matches on Sunday afternoons.

Tennis

Tennis was another sport popular from the early days in West Los Angeles. In 1887, the Santa Monica Improvement Company was formed as a civic group dedicated to bettering the community. Tennis was part of the improvement plan, and the group purchased land on Third Street near Washington

Avenue, building a clubhouse and courts. The courts hosted several major tournaments. Abbott Kinney, R.S. Baker and Gaylord Wilshire were all members and played tennis there. That same year, a Santa Monica resident won the Southern California championship on the first year it was held. May Carter captured the women's singles title three years running beginning with that win in 1887. Marion Jones, the daughter of Senator Jones, won the same title five times and then won the national women's singles title in 1899. She also won the national title in 1902, as well as several doubles titles.

The Sutton sisters were the next champions from the area. May and her sisters Ethel, Florence and Violet were born in England but came to Los Angeles as children. May Sutton won the women's championship in 1899 at the age of fourteen, and she or one of her sisters won it every year for the next seventeen years. Sutton won Wimbledon in 1905, the first non-British woman to win a singles title. She shocked the audience by rolling up her sleeves and wearing a skirt that showed her ankles—very daring for the day. In 1908, she was the first sports celebrity to reign as the Queen of the Rose Parade. In 1912, she married Tom Bundy, himself a championship tennis player. (She had always stated she would not marry a man who couldn't beat her at tennis.) She semi-retired to raise her four children—one of whom was also a champion tennis player. However, she taught tennis and played until she was eighty-seven, playing her last match just before her death in 1975.

The Bundys' daughter Dorothy "Dodo" Bundy Cheney also competed at the national and international level. In 1938, she was the first American to win the Australian women's singles title. She won 343 United States Tennis Association national titles, 20 Senior Grand Slams and was inducted into the International Tennis Hall of Fame in 2011. (Her mother was inducted in 1956.) She is still playing at age ninety-six.

Other tennis players from the area included Elizabeth "Bunny" Ryan and Mary Browne. Ryan is a legend at Wimbledon, having won a number of titles there in doubles and mixed doubles.

Alphonzo Bell started playing tennis on the courts his father built on their ranch at Bell Station in 1881. He continued playing at Occidental College, where he won the Pacific Coast Tennis Championship and was Inter-Collegiate Tennis Champion. After Bell left the seminary, he concentrated on his tennis career, winning two medals at the St. Louis Olympics—bronze for singles and silver for doubles. He was one of the first tennis players from Southern California to make his mark outside of California. He was ranked in the top ten players nationally—a first for a Southern Californian. His success did much to promote the area as a strong source of good tennis players. Bell continued to play tennis well into middle age and was a finalist of the Southern California's singles championship in 1914. He was thirty-nine years old at the time.

Tom Bundy was born in Santa Monica, part of the pioneering Bundy family. He won the U.S. National Championship in 1912, 1913 and 1914. In 1912, he married May Sutton. They both continued to play tennis for many years, and he often played with or against Bell. Bundy built the Los Angeles Tennis Club in 1920 near Melrose and Vine Avenues. Its clubhouse opened in 1927 and became popular with the movie set thanks to its proximity to the studios.

Gussie Moran was also from Santa Monica. In 1949, she continued the tradition of shocking the British audiences with her famous lace panties. Her tennis costume was so short that the panties showed—another first for Wimbledon. She earned the nickname of "Gorgeous Gussie" for her attention-getting garb. It was such a shock to the British that it sparked a debate in Parliament. She did not win the tournament but certainly made a splash and influenced tennis styles for women.

The Riviera Country Club added a tennis club in 1963 with twenty-four courts, a clubhouse and locker room; it is one of the leading tennis clubs on the West Coast. The other country clubs also offer tennis for their members. The Christine Reed Park in Santa Monica offers tennis courts for the public, as do many of the other parks in the area. Many of the homes in West Los Angeles have their own tennis courts as well.

Chapter 6
Stardust

West Los Angeles weather was and is the obvious draw for much of its popularity. So it is not a great surprise that the embryonic movie industry discovered making movies in the sun was more fun than in the winter in New York. By 1908, moviemakers were regularly trekking to the Santa Monica beach to film bathing beauties. The first studio to set up shop was Vitagraph in 1910. It rented land on Ocean Avenue for its studio. (The site was near the present-day Georgian Hotel.) The Kalem Company leased the old Southern Pacific station a year later, and Essanay found a home on the corner of Ocean Avenue and Santa Monica Boulevard.

The uninhibited moviemakers used the whole town as an impromptu set, stopping traffic and invading yards. Bystanders often found themselves cast as extras. Santa Monica was not exactly thrilled by these actions, but Santa Monica is the background for some of the first movies made in California. The studios moved on to Hollywood and other environs by 1915, but the employees and stars remained in force as residents, and production companies still use the leafy streets and upscale environment of West Los Angeles for backdrops.

On Location

Inceville

In addition to Santa Monica, Santa Inez Canyon in Pacific Palisades had been a moviemaking site since 1909. The outdoor scenes of *The Count of Monte Cristo* used the area under the bluffs as a location in 1909. In 1911,

Thomas Harper Ince found the area and leased approximately eighteen thousand acres in the canyon in order to use its picturesque seashore to mountain scenery in his movies.

Ince thought that Santa Inez Canyon was the perfect environment for the westerns he was making popular. Ince was inventing the western cowboy-and-Indian genre, and even before leasing the canyon, he had hired an entire Wild West show including a Sioux Indian tribe. He installed them on his new site in a specially built village. Ince proceeded to build a permanent set of backdrops, buildings and locations in Santa Inez that quickly became known as Inceville. At its height, it had seven hundred people who lived and worked at the facility, a post office and sets that replicated Switzerland, a Japanese village and many other locations. There was a ship off the coast for pirate movies and herds of horses and cattle for extras in westerns. The cowboys and Indians spent their time wrangling the livestock when they were not shooting. Ince was good at recruiting talent and was responsible for making Billie Burke, Douglas Fairbanks and many more actors into stars. Max Sennett made movies at Inceville with Charlie Chaplin and Mable Normand. At its height in 1915, Inceville's payroll was $85,000 a month.

When extras were needed for a project, Ince advertised a "grand fiesta and barbeque." Residents were thrilled to come up the coast for a free lunch and a chance to be in the movies. Arthur Loomis used to recount how he played hooky from school in order to earn the five bucks and lunch. Borrowing his future wife's (Dorothy Gillis) horse and donning an Indian costume, he found himself charging down the cliffs in a scene eventually used in *Custer's Last Fight.* To his embarrassment, he lost his seat on the horse and fell off, spectacularly. He was offered ten dollars to repeat his stunt the next day, but he declined, ending his movie career. Twenty-five thousand extras were needed for Ince's 1918 film *Civilization.* That film was an ambitious undertaking pleading for peace. However, it was ultimately for naught. It was cancelled when the United States entered the war in 1917 at a huge loss for Ince. Inceville was eventually doomed when Ince built a large indoor studio in Culver City in 1915. In 1916, a fire destroyed many of the buildings at Inceville and injured Ince and a number of the other workers.

Ince had planned to continue using both Inceville and his studio in Culver City, but it gradually lost its popularity with the studios. It burned to the ground once and for all in 1922.

Ince

Thomas Harper Ince was born into a stage family—his father was a comedian and his mother was an actress—in Newport, Rhode Island. Both his brothers also became film directors. He started out directing films in New York in 1907 after trying his hand on the stage. Ince was an innovator who developed many of the procedures needed to mass-produce movies for the burgeoning public demand. The property he leased north of Santa Monica at Santa Inez Canyon was one of the first permanent studio sites.

Ince continued to make movies and innovate for the industry until his untimely and mysterious death in 1924. Ince was negotiating with William Randolph Hearst to use some of Hearst's magazines' stories for movies; Hearst wanted Ince to direct Marion Davies in her upcoming roles. The men were planning on finalizing these agreements and celebrating Ince's birthday on Hearst's yacht in San Diego. Ince joined Hearst's other guests, including Marion Davies and Charlie Chaplin, for the evening party. The rest of the story remains a mystery.

The official story was that Ince was stricken with "indigestion," and his wife was summoned to take him home the next day. Later that day Ince, by then attended by his own doctor, suffered a stroke and died. His body was immediately cremated. And then the rumors flew, the most interesting one being that in a drunken bout of jealousy, Hearst mistook Ince for Chaplin, whom he thought he had seen in an embrace with Davies, and shot him. Another version was that Hearst intended to shoot Ince because he thought Ince was having an affair with Davies. One other variation was that Davies, in a drunken rage over Hearst's jealousy, brought the gun on deck and threatened suicide. Ince struggled with her trying to get the gun away and was shot by mistake. Everyone on the deck thought it was a prop gun that fired blanks, but it was a real pistol. The investigation was cursory, and since no one is alive today to ask, the mystery will remain unsolved.

Movie Stars

William Randolph Hearst

William Randolph Hearst was born in San Francisco, the son of a wealthy mining engineer, in 1863. He was educated at Harvard although he was expelled for outrageous pranks. In 1887, he took over the *San Francisco*

William Randolph Hearst in 1906. He was a member of the House of Representatives for New York at this time.

Examiner for his father, who had acquired it as payment for a poker debt. His brand of sensational journalism and the talented writers—Jack London, Mark Twain and Ambrose Bierce—he hired made the paper popular and increased circulation. After the San Francisco earthquake in 1906, he hired Julia Morgan to design a new building for the company—her first big commission. In 1895, Hearst bought the *New York Morning Journal* and applied the same formula to turn it into a high-circulation paper. He purchased a number of papers and magazines across the country, eventually owning the biggest publishing company in the United States. One of the papers he owned was the *Los Angeles Examiner*. He also owned radio stations and a film company. His other interests included land in California and Mexico, New York real estate and timber and mining. He was elected to Congress from New York in 1903, ran for mayor of New York in 1905 and 1909 (losing both elections) and also lost a try for governor of New York in 1906.

Giving up on politics, Hearst became involved with starlet Marion Davies. While he remained married to his wife, he lived openly with Davies after 1919.

One of Hearst's passions was building, and he began building Hearst Castle on his ranch at San Simeon in 1919. In 1926, he began construction on a beach house on the Gold Coast in Santa Monica. Julia Morgan worked on the beach house and made it a landmark on the Santa Monica beach. It is estimated to have cost $7 million. Hearst and Davies lavishly entertained the Hollywood elite there during the 1930s.

Hearst and Alphonzo Bell crossed paths when Hearst wanted to purchase land in Bel-Air to build a home for Davies (the home that he eventually built

Marion Davies as she must have looked when she and W.R. Hearst became involved in their long-standing relationship.

on the Gold Coast). Bell was well known for his strict religious views and refused to sell him the land because he disapproved both of the movies and of Hearst's open affair with Davies. That decision earned Hearst's wrath, which would haunt Bell in later years. The *Los Angeles Examiner* opposed Bell when he tried to open a quarry and cement plant in Pacific Palisades, fueling a long-running and expensive legal battle for Bell. The paper also sensationalized an auto accident that involved Bell's daughter. Hearst was a larger-than-life figure, and he influenced many issues with his prejudices and enthusiasms.

Marion Davies

Marion Davies was a twenty-year-old with a growing reputation for comedy when she became known for her relationship with William Randolph Hearst. Davies was born in New York near Battery Park and changed her name from Douras to Davies when she became a Ziegfield girl. She starred in her first feature movie in 1917 and the following year did three more. Her roles in light comedy quickly made her popular. Hearst made it his personal project to further her career, forming Cosmopolitan Pictures to produce her films. His obsession with her career seems to have been more harmful than helpful, forcing her to take roles that did not suit her bubbly personality.

The advent of "talkies" were a challenge for Davies as she tended to stutter, but she continued to work in comedies and musicals during the '30s. Hearst's interference in her career often led to retaliation through his newspapers when she was denied a role he had lobbied for her. She made her last picture in 1937 and retired in conjunction with the demise of Hearst's Cosmopolitan Pictures. Critics of the time (who did not work for Hearst) panned her work, but today's opinion is that she was a talented actress, especially in her comedic roles.

Perhaps her most important role was as Hearst's lover and mistress of some thirty years. Hearst never divorced his wife, apparently finding the settlement terms too expensive, but he lived openly with Davies from 1919

The Davies house was used for lavish entertainments and costume parties, with many movie stars and moguls in attendance. *Left to right:* Jack Warner, Raul Walsh, Marion Davies, W.R. Hearst and Mrs. Raul Welsh. *Courtesy of the University of Southern California on behalf of the USC Special Collections.*

until his death in 1951. As a couple, they entertained lavishly at all of their various homes—San Simeon, St. Donat's Castle in Wales and the lavish beach house located on the Gold Coast at Santa Monica. The parties were extravagant, and invitations were prized by everyone in the business and movie worlds. Their lifestyle and idiosyncrasies inspired numerous movies and plays, including Orson Welles's *Citizen Kane*. Hearst fought the distribution of *Citizen Kane* supposedly to protect Davies's reputation. By the end of the 1930s, Hearst was financially and physically failing. St. Donat's was sold, and it is rumored that at one point Davies had to loan him money. At his death in 1951, he left her 51 percent of his estate. After Hearst's death, Davies married Horace Brown and became involved in charity work, donating money to establish a children's hospital at UCLA (now Mattel Children's Hospital) and money to fight other childhood diseases through her foundation. Her name survives as part of the UCLA medical center. She died in 1961.

Julia Morgan

Julia Morgan was born in San Francisco in 1874. She received a civil engineering degree from Berkeley, and she was one of the first women to gain a diploma from L'Ecole des Beaux-Arts in Paris. She is generally considered the first female architect in California. Morgan lived most of her life in San Francisco, and most of her more than seven hundred buildings are in that area, but her association with William Randolph Hearst brought her to Santa Monica to design his beach house for Marion Davies. Morgan met Hearst's mother, Phoebe Apperson Hearst, while she was working on the University of California at Berkeley campus. Hearst was a patron of the university, and it is believed she introduced Morgan to her son. Her first commission for Hearst was the *Los Angeles Examiner* building. She went on to design Hearst Castle and several other estates for Hearst. Morgan is known for integrating the symmetry of the Beaux Arts School with the architectural vocabulary of the West. Her style is a combination of these influences.

She designed the beach house for Hearst and Marion Davies in 1926. Located on the Santa Monica Gold Coast, the property had

Marion Davies's beach house, designed by Julia Morgan, dominates the beach. After Davies sold the house, it was used briefly as hotel. Most of the structure was torn down in the 1940s, and only the guesthouse remains. It is currently the Annenberg Community Beach House, a beach club offering access to the public with no membership required.

several houses, a large pool and 110 rooms. Morgan managed to harmonize these elements into a pleasant backdrop for Hearst's lavish lifestyle. The white-pillared house was Davies's home from 1929 to 1942. The house was sold in 1942, and most of it was torn down. The remaining guesthouse has been through several transitions but is now the Annenberg Community Beach House and is open to the public.

Leo Carrillo

Leopoldo Antonio Carrillo was a well-known stage and movie actor during the 1920s and '30s and of course is best known for his last role as Pancho in *The Cisco Kid* TV series. He was born in an adobe house in Los Angeles and raised in Santa Monica. He was related to both the Bandinis and the Sepulvedas, as well as many other Californio families. (His Bandini cousin Peggy Loomis used to reminisce about how he serenaded her with "Peg-O-My Heart" from the Broadway stage when he discovered she was in the audience.) The Carrillo family came to California in 1749 with Portola's expedition and included a governor of Alta California, a three-time mayor of Los Angeles and numerous other landholders and prominent historical figures. His father, Juan Jose Carrillo, was the chief of police in Santa Monica and its first mayor. He was also a judge.

Carrillo's show business career launched when he subbed in for a missing act on the Orpheum Circuit. His line of patter and mimicry was a hit. His talent for accents landed him roles such as Tony, a comic Italian in the play *Twin Beds.* One of his plays ran for two years on Broadway, and he toured with the play internationally. After that gig, he made his way home to Los Angeles to make movies. He was very successful in that genre as well. Carrillo built his home, Los Alisos (the Sycamores), in the early 1920s on three lots in Santa Monica Canyon and often entertained his friends there. Early on, the parties at the California-style house had to end at dusk because there was no power in the area yet.

In addition to his acting career, Carrillo was active as both a preservationist and a conservationist. He actively considered running for governor of California in 1941 but bowed out in favor of his friend Earl Warren. As part of the California Beach and Parks Commission (appointed by Warren), he helped to acquire Hearst Castle for the state and the Anza Borrego Desert State Park. Leo Carrillo State Beach Park, west of Malibu, is named for him. He was a great favorite at parades for many years, riding Conquistador, his Palomino horse. He also built an adobe ranch retreat in San Diego near the property once owned by his Bandini ancestors. Before his death, he wrote a memoir entitled *The California I Love* that is a wonderful tale of both his life and life in early twentieth-century West Los Angeles. He died in 1961.

Will Rogers

One of William Penn Adair Rogers's best friends from his vaudeville days was Leo Carrillo. In fact, Carrillo says in his book that he was the one who convinced Rogers to retool his act around his cowboy persona with roping and humorous political patter. Carrillo also convinced Rogers to locate his ranch across the canyon from Carrillo's property in Santa Monica Canyon.

Rogers was born in the Indian Territory (soon to be Oklahoma) to a prominent Cherokee family. He was about one-quarter Cherokee, and one of his better lines became, "My ancestors didn't come over on the *Mayflower*; they met the boat." His father was a prominent leader in the Cherokee community and a very successful rancher. Rogers dropped out of school in the tenth grade to pursue his interests—riding, roping and horses.

After several failed business ventures, he signed on as a trick roper with Texas Jack's Wild West Circus, a competitor of Wild Bill Cody's Wild West extravaganzas. A chance encounter with a runaway steer in Madison Square Garden—he roped it—gave him the publicity needed to make the leap to vaudeville. Rogers married his wife in 1908 and moved to the Ziegfield Follies in 1916. His act consisted of him dressed in cowboy gear twirling his rope and commenting on the headlines of the day. He made his first silent film in New York in 1918. Samuel Goldwyn signed him to a three-year contract at triple what he was making in New York, and Rogers came west. Silent films could not showcase his talent for commentary, and he did not become a true movie star until "talkies" became the norm after 1929.

He made twenty-one films. At the same time, he toured on the lecture circuit—becoming perhaps the world's first frequent flyer—and wrote a weekly newspaper column. He published books of his jokes and commentary. His wit and personality made him everyone's friend, from the man on the street to the president of the United States. With the advent of radio, he became an on-air personality. His weekly Sunday evening show—*The Gulf Headliners*—became a top-ranked program.

Rogers's ranch north of Santa Monica became a mecca for movie celebrities and other luminaries. They gathered on Sunday mornings to play polo or rode with Rogers on the many trails he laid out over his ranch. He built a home there and also a large barn—big enough to practice roping on wet days. Rogers was an early and enthusiastic fan of aviation. He made his lecture tour work by flying with the crews carrying the mail from coast to coast. He was friends with Charles Lindbergh and an advocate for the system of passenger airlines developing in Europe. His advocacy for what he considered the future of transportation was instrumental in its success. In 1935, on a trip to Alaska with aviator Wiley Post, the two men were killed in an airplane crash.

At his wife's death, Rogers's ranch was donated to the state as a park, and there are many schools, airports and other memorials to Will Rogers. One of them is the Will Rogers State Beach at the mouth of Santa Monica Canyon. Rogers had bought the beach frontage in the 1920s, planning to subdivide it as an extension of the Gold Coast. (He sold lots to Hearst for the Davies beach house.) At his death, it was heavily mortgaged to the Santa Monica Land & Water Company. Eventually R.C. Gillis forgave the debt, and Rogers's wife donated the land to the state to be used as a beach. It is a lasting reminder to the Westside of his presence in the area. It is also a fitting tribute to these two friends—Leo Carrillo and Will Rogers—that the beaches named for them are at opposite ends of the same beach.

Chapter 7

ROUNDUP

It is a cliché, but true—change is the only constant. West Los Angeles proves its truth. Change has characterized the area for over one hundred years—open land has been transformed from rancho to homes and streets; cattle and sheep have given way to residents and tourists; Native American canoes have been replaced by surfboards; horses are rare and only one polo field has survived; railroads and trolleys have been replaced by automobiles; only one pleasure pier remains; and cottages have become McMansions. The list of transformations is long. However, there is also a long list of enduring and familiar attractions—the weather, the ocean, the hills and canyons, the sun, the gardens full of flowering plants, the golf courses, the tennis courts, the energetic people and their imaginative ideas. Together, this mix of change and familiar ensures that West Los Angeles continues to evolve and remains a fun, hip, interesting and fascinating place to live. There will be more tales to tell.

Bibliography

Books

Bandini, Helen Elliot. *History of California*. New York: American Book Company, 1908.

Basten, Fred E. *Santa Monica Bay, The First 100 Years*. Los Angeles: Douglas-West Publishers, Inc., 1974.

———. *Santa Monica Bay: A Pictorial History of Santa Monica, Venice, Ocean Park, Marina del Rey, Pacific Palisades, Topanga & Malibu*. Santa Monica, CA: Hennessey and Ingalls, 1997.

Beebe, Rose Marie, and Robert M. Senkewicz. *Lands of Promise and Despair*. Santa Clara, CA: Santa Clara University & Heyday Books, Berkeley, 2001.

———. *Testimonios—Early California through the Eyes of Women*. Berkeley: Bancroft Library, University of California, 2006.

Bell, Alphonzo, Jr. *The Bel-Air Kid, An Autobiography of a Life in California*. Victoria, BC: Trafford Publishing, 2002.

Bundy, Vivian Mayo. *Meet Our Ancestors*. Greensboro, NC: Media, Inc., 1978.

Carrillo, Leo. *The California I Love*. Englewood Cliffs, CA: Prentice-Hall, 1961.

Cleland, Robert Glass. *The Cattle on a Thousand Hills: Southern California, 1850–80*. San Marino, CA: Huntington Library, 1990.

———. *Pathfinders*, Vol. I, of the IX Vol. series *California*. Edited by John Russell McCarthy. Los Angeles: Powell Publishing Company, 1928.

Crosby, Harry W. *Gateway to Alta California: The Expedition to San Diego, 1769*. San Diego, CA: Sunbelt Publications, 2003.

Drinkwater, Judy, and Jan Loomis. *A Datebook for the Westsiders of Los Angeles: 1982*. Los Angeles: Santa Monica Bay Printing and Publishing Company, 1981.

———. *Yesterday Tripping: 1984*. Los Angeles: Santa Monica Bay Printing and Publishing Company, 1984.

Dukesherer, D.J. *Playa Del Rey: The Early History of Playa Del Rey, Westchester, and Playa Vista California*. Los Angeles: Central Historical Group Publishing, 2010.

Dumke, Glenn S. *The Boom of the Eighties in Southern California*. San Marino, CA: Huntington Library, 1944.

Editorial staff of *Sunset Magazine*. *Sunset Western Ranch Houses*. San Francisco: Lane Publishing Company, 1950.

Fogelson, Robert M. *The Fragmented Metropolis: Los Angeles, 1850–1930*. Berkeley: University of California Press, 1967.

Gates, Russell, ed. *Bel-Air Bay Club, A Country Place by the Sea*. Pacific Palisades, CA: The Bel-Air Bay Club, Ltd., 1997.

Gorham, Harry M. *My Memories of The Comstock*. Los Angeles: Suttonhouse Publishers, 1939.

Graves, Jackson A. *California Memories, 1857–1930*. Los Angeles: Times Mirror Press, 1930.

———. *My Seventy Years in California, 1857–1927*. Los Angeles: Times-Mirror Press, 1929.

Gross, Michael. *Unreal Estate*. New York: Broadway Books, 2011.

Harris, James. *Santa Monica Pier: A Century on the Last Great Pleasure Pier*. Santa Monica, CA: Angel City Press, 2009.

Harrison, Gilbert A. *A Timeless Affair, the Life of Anita McCormack Blaine*. Chicago: University of Chicago Press, 1979.

Hayes, Benjamin Judge. *Pioneer Notes from the Diaries of Judge Benjamin Hayes*. Los Angeles: privately printed, 1929.

Horton, Joseph K. *A Brief History of Bel-Air.* Bel-Air, CA: The Bel-Air Association, 1982.

Ingersoll, Luther A. *Ingersoll's Century History, Santa Monica Bay Cities*. Los Angeles: Luther Ingersoll, 1909.

Johnson, Hank. *Rails to the Minarets: The Story of the Sugar Pine Lumber Company*. Fish Camp, CA: Stauffer Publishing, 2011.

Johnson, Paul, and staff of *Sunset Magazine*. *Western Ranch Houses by Cliff May*. Menlo Park, CA: Lane Publishing Company, 1958.

Kauffman, Henry J. *The Pennsylvania Kentucky Rifle.* Morgantown, PA: Masthof Press, 2005.

Loomis, Jan. *Images of America: Brentwood*. Mount Pleasant, SC: Arcadia Publishing, 2008.

———. *Images of America: Pacific Palisades*. Mount Pleasant, SC: Arcadia Publishing, 2009.

Marquez, Earnest. *Noir Afloat: Tony Cornero and the Notorious Gambling Ships of Southern California*. Santa Monica, CA: Angel City Press, 2011.

———. *Port of Los Angeles, A Phenomenon of the Railroad Era*. San Marino, CA: Golden West Books, 1975.

———. *Santa Monica Beach, A Collector's Pictorial History*. Santa Monica, CA: Angel City Press, 2004.

Mason, William Marvin. *Census of 1790: A Demographic History of Colonial California*. Menlo Park, CA: Ballena Press, 1998.

McGroarty, John Steven. *Los Angeles, From the Mountains to the Sea, Vol.I–IV*. Chicago: American Historical Society, 1921.

Mitchell, Sydney B. *Gardening in California: A Guide for the Amateur on the Pacific Slope*. Garden City, NY: Doubleday, Page and Company, 1925.

Myers, William A., and Ira L. Swett. *Trolleys to the Surf: The Story of the Los Angeles Pacific Railway*. Glendale, CA: Interurban Publications, 1976.

Newmark, Harris. *Sixty Years in Southern California, 1853–1913*. New York: Knickerbocker Press, 1926.

Northrop, Marie E. *Spanish-Mexican Families of Early California: 1769–1850, Vol. I.* Burbank: Southern California Genealogical Society, 1987.

———. *Spanish-Mexican Families of Early California: 1769–1850, Vol. II.* Burbank: Southern California Genealogical Society, 1984.

Northrop, Marie E., and William M. Mason. *Spanish-Mexican Families of Early California: Vol. III—Los Pobladores de la Reina de Los Angeles*. Burbank: Southern California Genealogical Society, 2004.

Osmer, Harold, and Phil Harms. *Real Road Racing: The Santa Monica Road Races*. Chatsworth, CA: Harold L. Osmer Publishing, 1999.

Padilla, Victoria. *Southern California Gardens: An Illustrated History*. Berkeley: University of California Press, 1961.

Pourade, Richard F. *The Silver Dons*. San Diego, CA: Union-Tribune Publishing Company, 1963.

Read, Nat B. *The Jonathan Club Story*. Los Angeles: Balcony Press, 2005.

Rindge, Frederick H. *Happy Days in Southern California, Cambridge, Massachusetts and Los Angeles, California*. Los Angeles: Malibu Historical Society, 1972.

Rosen, Lou. *Henry Gaylord Wilshire: The Millionaire Socialist*. Pacific Palisades, CA: School Justice Institute, 2011.

Sitton, Tom, and William Deverall, eds. *Metropolis in the Making: Los Angeles in the 1920s*. Berkeley: University of California Press, 2001.

White, Carl F., ed. *Santa Monica Community Book, Fifth Edition*. Santa Monica, CA: A.H. Cawston, 1953.

Young, Betty Lou. *Pacific Palisades, Where the Mountains Meet the Sea*. Pacific Palisades, CA: Pacific Palisades Historical Society, 1983.

———. *Rustic Canyon and the Story of the Uplifters*. Santa Monica, CA: Casa Vieja Press, 1975.

Young, Randy, and Betty Lou Young. *Street Names of Pacific Palisades and Other Tales*. Pacific Palisades, CA: Pacific Palisades Historical Society, 1990.

Online Sources

Crosse, John. *Playa del Rey: Speed Capital of the World, the Los(t) Angeles Motordome, 1910–1913*. Southern California Architectural History, Blog, http://socalarchhistory.blogspot.com/2011/03/first-board-track-opened-at-los-angeles.html.

The Electric Railway Historical Association of Southern California. *Los Angeles Pacific, Balloon Route Excursion*. http://www.erha.org/balloon.htm.

Garden City Company of California. *1916 Ideal Homes in Garden Communities*. Various articles. http://www.antiquehomestyle.com/plans/garden-city-co/index.htm.

Mid Century Home, Case Study House #20: *The Richard Neutra Baily House*. http://www.mid-century-home.com/case-study-house-program/case-study-house-20-the-richard-neutra-baily-house/.

Pacific Coast Architecture Database (PCAD). Various articles. https://digital.lib.washington.edu/architects.

Pohlman, John O. "Alphonzo E. Bell: A Biography: Part I." *Southern California Quarterly* 46, no. 3 (September 1964): 197–222. Berkeley and Los Angeles: Published by University of California Press on behalf of the Historical Society of Southern California, 1964. Accessed: May 23, 2012 19:07. http://www.jstor.org/stable/41169866.

———. "Alphonzo E. Bell: A Biography: Part II." *Southern California Quarterly* 46, no. 4 (December 1964): 315–50. Berkeley and Los Angeles: Published by University of California Press on behalf of the Historical Society of Southern California, 1964. Accessed: May 23, 2012 19:25. http://www.jstor.org/stable/41171357.

San Diego History Center. Various articles. http://www.sandiegohistory.org.
Wikipedia, The Free Encyclopedia. Various articles. http://en.wikipedia.org.

Periodicals

Bates, Colleen Dunn. "Sunset Roulette." *Previews, A Community Magazine* 7, no. 3 (March 1986): 14–19.
Kidd, Nina. "Cliff May, California Ranch House Designer." *Previews, A Community Magazine* 7, no. 7 (July 1986): 17–22.
———. "Crestwood Hills." *Previews, A Community Magazine* 8, no. 4 (April 1987): 18–23.
———. "Haciendas on the Westside." *Previews, A Community Magazine* 6, no. 5 (May 1986): 18–22.
———. "Mandeville Canyon: Rustic Past, Clouded Future." *Previews, A Community Magazine* 9, no. 4 (April 1988): 24–25.
Loomis, Jan. "LA West Salutes the West Los Angeles Veterans' Administration Medical Center, 1888–1988: A Century of Caring." *L.A. West* 9, no. 5 (May 1988): 33–48.
MacDowell, Don. "Trolley to the Sea." *Previews, A Community Magazine* 7, no. 4 (April 1986): 18–21.

Unpublished Sources

Loomis, Robert G. "Huntington Palisades." A paper submitted to satisfy the requirement for BA-182U.C.L.A. 1956.
Minutes, Executive Committee, Pacific Land Corporation. Santa Monica Land & Water Co. Archives. 1929–1932.
Minutes, Pacific Land Corporation, 3 Volumes. Santa Monica Land & Water Co. Archives. 1928–1937.
Minutes, Santa Monica Land & Water Co., 5 Volumes. Santa Monica Land & Water Co. Archives. 1897–1989.
Santa Monica Land & Water Company Archives. 1897–1983.

Index

F

G

H

I

J

K

L

M

N

T

V

W

About the Author

A fascination with old photographic images led Jan Loomis to her interest in the development of West Los Angeles. The photographs were part of the records of the Santa Monica Land & Water Company (SML&WCo). Incorporated in 1897, the company was in existence for almost one hundred years and was responsible for creating many of the communities that make up West Los Angeles. Loomis has a background in art, history, publishing and electronic information delivery. She has a degree in fine art from Scripps College in Claremont, California, with a minor in humanities. Her discovery of the extensive files of the SML&WCo led her to train as an archivist as well.

Her career has included stints as an editor and publisher of magazines and newsletters. She has also developed numerous electronic information sites for both publishers and dot-com companies. Loomis has published many articles about local Los Angeles history and about electronic content. She is also a frequent speaker at historical associations and library groups in West Los Angeles. On a personal note, she has been married to her husband, Bob Loomis, who is related to most of the people mentioned in this book, for almost fifty years and has five grandchildren whom she hopes will eventually come to know where their ancestors lived and worked through her writing. Her other books include *Images of America: Brentwood* and *Images of America: Pacific Palisades.*